The Enemies List

The Enemies List

Compiled by
P. J. O'Rourke

with Contributions from
the Readers of *The American Spectator*

THE ATLANTIC MONTHLY PRESS
NEW YORK

"Why I Am a Conservative in the First Place" was first published in
Rolling Stone. All the other pieces in this book originally appeared, sometimes
in slightly different form and with different titles, in *The American Spectator*.
"A Call for a New McCarthyism" was also published in *Give War a Chance*,
and "100 Reasons Why Jimmy Carter Was a Better President Than
Bill Clinton" in *Age and Guile Beat Youth, Innocence, and a Bad Haircut*
(both Atlantic Monthly Press).

First edition

Printed in the United States of America

Library of Congress Cataloging-in-Publication Data

O'Rourke, P. J.
The enemies list / compiled by P. J. O'Rourke; with contributions
by the readers of The American spectator. — 1st ed.
p.   cm.
ISBN 0-87113-632-5
I.   The American spectator.   II.   Title.
PN6162.O74   1996
818'.540208—dc20   96-4887

Illustrations by John Springs

To subscribe to the *American Spectator* send a check for $29.95 for 12 monthly
issues to: *The American Spectator*, P. J. O'Rourke Offer, P.O. Box 657,
Mt. Morris, IL 61054 or call toll free: 1-800-524-3469 and mention this
offer: PJ0496

Atlantic Monthly Press
841 Broadway
New York, NY 10003

10 9 8 7 6 5 4 3 2 1

To my Grandmother

Edna Olive Loy

*Who could never understand why people worried
about communism when there were so many
Democrats still to be jailed*

≪Contents≫

❖

≪ Introduction ≫

by Wladyslaw Pleszczynski,
Executive Editor, *The American Spectator*

"Have you no decency, sir?" the infamous Joseph Welch asked Senator Joseph McCarthy on June 9, 1954, setting the idea of witch-hunts back some thirty-five years. What's been forgotten is that Senator Joe was never given a chance to respond, which has always bothered P. J. O'Rourke. He'd long felt a natural affinity for the Tail-Gunner—these two Irish Midwesterners, after all, share the same November birthday. Besides, it really sets him off when somebody calls somebody else "sir." There was also the question of proportion. No matter how crocked Senator Joe might have been that day, he certainly displayed greater decency in his condition than Welch did in his coddling of card-carrying pinkos. So by the time P.J. reached his forties—the same age that saw McCarthy come into his prime—he was ready to roll. With the Berlin Wall about to crumble, he saw an opening and issued his Call for a New McCarthyism.

And this time it would be done right. When Joe launched his campaign by waving a sheet of paper said to contain the names of 205 Communists in the State Department, he did so before the Ohio Valley Women's Republican Club of Wheeling, West Virginia, and then he turned to J. Edgar Hoover and his G-men for help in coming up with more names. When P.J. issued his "Plea for a Renewed Red Scare," he did so by listing a random sample of parlor pinks and public enemies in the pages of the *American Spectator* of Arlington, Virginia, and—allowing his political genius to take over—he turned to the readers of this publication for help in coming up with more names.

The result was a spirited outpouring against the rogues and rakes in our midst that gave way to a new Era of Good Feelings. Talking back to the libs was good, clean, enlightening fun. Long before it became fashionable to practice community involvement, readers were finding fishy characters in every nook and cranny of their lives—in the schools and universities that indoctrinated them, in the newspapers, magazines, and books that propagandized them, in the local and national news that insulted them, in the television programs and movies they fell asleep watching. And they were sharing it all with P.J., who would reward them next time around with a listing of names and aliases from his latest roundup of shirkers, shrinkers, and outlaws. Long before anyone had ever heard of and forgotten about "politics of meaning" guru Michael Lerner, P.J. was fingering Lerner's magazine *Tikkun*. He fought to defund the Left long before anyone had ever heard of Newt Gingrich. He understood that in an age of whiny wimps, ridicule is all you need. Or to put it another way: Live free or else.

In all, O'Rourke McCarthyism was setting the stage for the likes of Rush Limbaugh and the rest of the talk radio movement. And it also proved a Sisyphean labor. P.J. and friends may have been shooting fish in a barrel—but the damn thing kept expanding, so that by 1993, the final year of the list, it was big enough to contain not only Bill Clinton but his first wife, the veep's wife, Donna Shalala, and many of their friends. Hot damn, an Arkansas hot tub!

The experience has left P.J. more philosophical than ever. It's even given him a new appreciation of Jimmy Carter, carpenter and former president of the United States.

January 5, 1996
Arlington, Virginia

❖

<< I >>

A Call for a
New McCarthyism

The American Spectator, July 1989

S prings

O ur era is supposed to be the 1950s all over again. Indeed, we are experiencing anew many of the pleasures and benefits of that excellent decade: a salubrious prudery, a sensible avariciousness, a healthy dose of social conformity, a much-needed narrowing of minds, and a return to common-sense American political troglodytism. But there's one delightful and entertaining feature of the Eisenhower years which is wholly absent from the contemporary scene—old-fashioned red-baiting. Where's our McCarthyism? Who's our Tail-Gunner Joe? Why don't we get to look for Communists under our beds or—considering the social changes of the past thirty-five years—*in* them? ("Good night, honey, and are you now or have you ever been a member of the Committee in Solidarity with the People of El Salvador?")

God knows the problem is not a lack of Commies. There are more fuzzy-minded one-worlders, pasty-faced peace creeps, and bleeding-heart bed wetters in America now than there ever were in 1954. The redskis have infiltrated the all-important exercise-video industry, not to mention movies and TV. Academia, too, is a veritable compost heap of Bolshie brainmulch. Beardo the Weirdo may have been laughed out of real life during the 1970s, but he found a home in our nation's colleges, where he whiles away the wait for the next Woodstock Nation by pestering undergraduates with collectivist twaddle when they should be thinking about better car stereos. And fellow travelers in the State Department? Jeez, the situation is so bad at Foggy Bottom that we'd better *hope* it's caused by spies. If it's stupidity, we're really in trouble.

So how come the HUAC staff isn't returning my phone calls? Who's keeping *I Led Three Lives* from being remade starring Tom Selleck and Arnold Schwarzenegger? And why aren't we making sure that that Fidel-snuggler Ron Dellums never works again? Whoops, we already did that. We elected him to Congress. And come to think of it, there are other problems with an up-to-date nineties-style witch-hunt. For one thing, it's no use going after real, card-carrying Communists anymore. Hard-core party *apparatchiks* have already been persecuted by organizations more brutally efficient than anything we've got in the U.S., organizations such as the Union of Soviet Socialist Republics. Plus, accusing somebody of being a "comsymp" just isn't the same since Gorbachev began his three-hankie perestroika performance. Even Margaret Thatcher says she sympathized with Ole Splotch-Top. And when it comes to the International Communist Conspiracy to Enslave Europe, Asia, and the Third World—well, somebody's got to do *something* with those people. Good luck to the Patrice Lumumba University Class of '89.

No, a modern McCarthyism is going to have to concentrate on other things besides the Big Lie and the Red Menace. In fact, if we examine even a brief selection of people who should be tarred and feathered and run out of town on a rail (or, to be more contemporary, oat branned and goose downed and jogged out of the condominium complex on an exercise track), we see that they are not necessarily Marxist or even socialist in their thinking because that would presuppose thinking in the first place. Nobody is ever going to accuse us of being *thought* police for going after the likes of Kris Kristofferson, Phil Donahue, Marlo Thomas, Dr. Benjamin Spock, Yoko Ono, Dave Dellinger, Ben and Jerry's Ice Cream, the World Council of Churches, Ed Asner, Michelle Shocked, Lenora Fulani, Robert Redford, and people who think quartz crystals cure herpes.

The distinguishing feature of this cluster of dunces is not subversion but silliness. If we hope to wreck careers, destroy reputations, and drive holistic Ortega fans into exile in Sausalito and Amherst, we're going to need tactics very different from those used by Roy Cohn, Bobby Kennedy, and the distinguished senator from the great state famous for its La Follette and cheese. A "blacklist" will never work. Put some Sandalista on your blacklist and you probably guarantee him a MacArthur genius grant and a seat on the ACLU national board of directors. But maybe we can tear a page from the *Très Riches Heures* of Tipper Gore and insist upon a rating system for music, film, television, and the *Boston Globe* editorial page. A warning would have to be prominently displayed: "OH-OH, A PERSON INVOLVED WITH THIS UNAPPEALING ITEM OF MASS COMMUNICATION HOLDS SILLY OPINIONS ON MATTERS ABOUT WHICH HE OR SHE IS LARGELY OR ABYSMALLY UNINFORMED." There'd be three ratings:

S = Silly
VS = Very Silly
SML = Shirley MacLaine

Thus a rerun of *M*A*S*H* featuring Alan Alda would get an "S" rating. Any public pronouncement by a member of the innumerable Phoenix family, such as River, Leaf, Summer, Stump, Ditch, or Pond Scum Phoenix, would get a "VS" rating. And the new Tracy Chapman album gets an "SML" with oak-leaf cluster.

But, no, this isn't going to work either. You can't shame or humiliate modern celebrities. What used to be called shame and humiliation is now called publicity. And forget traditional character assassination. If you say a modern celebrity is an adulterer, a pervert, and a drug addict, all it means is that you've read his autobiography.

We have to come up with more clever ways to ruin these people. Perhaps we can spread rumors that they performed in South Africa. I was in South Africa myself a few years ago, and I'm almost certain that was Jessica Mitford singing backup for Frank Sinatra at Sun City. Or perhaps we can direct the wrath of the remarkably terrifying animal rights activists against them. I'm going to write a letter to People for the Ethical Treatment of Animals about how Susan Sontag allows her ideas to be tried on innocent laboratory rabbits before humans are exposed to them. (As for the animal rights activists, we can turn some animals loose on them later.)

But the worst punishment for dupes, pink-wieners, and dialectical immaterialists might be a kind of reverse blacklist. We don't prevent them from writing, speaking, performing, and otherwise being their usual nuisance selves. Instead, we hang on their every word, beg them to work, drag them onto all available TV and radio chat shows, and write hundreds of fawning newspaper and magazine articles about their wonderful swellness. In other words, we subject them to the monstrous, gross, and irreversible late-twentieth-century phenomenon of Media Overexposure so that a surfeited public rebels in disgust. This is the "Pia Zadora Treatment," and, for condemning people to obscurity, it beats the Smith Act hollow.

Anyway, I'm sure we'll find some way to chastise these buggers of sense, to bully, torment, harry them, and generally make a workers' paradise of their lives. In the meantime, the fun part of McCarthyism is, as it always was, *making out the enemies list.* Heh-heh:

> *Sting*
> *Gore Vidal*
> *The Institute for Policy Studies*
> *Tom Hayden* (Hope you didn't give Jane your ideals in the divorce
>   settlement, Tom.)
> *Victor Navasky*
> *Angela Davis*
> *William Sloane Coffin*
> *Noam Chomsky*
> *Abbie Hoffman* (I guess we can cross him off; he was on God's list.)

Ralph Nader

Anthony Lewis

William "The Client Is Obviously Guilty" Kunstler

Jackson Browne

Allen Ginsberg

Norman Lear

Meryl Streep

Peter, Paul and Mary (Yes, they're still alive.)

The Christic Institute

Common Cause

Center for Constitutional Rights

Anybody whose last name is Cockburn

Anybody who inherited so much money and so little sense that her last name might become Cockburn

Cockburn wannabe Christopher Hitchens (Who's checking the green cards around here?)

The Order of Maryknoll Nuns

Amy Carter

Susan Sarandon

The Redgrave family

Patty Duke

Casey Kasem

Daniel and Philip Berrigan (Yes, *they're* still alive, too.)

Mike Farrell

Tikkun

The Progressive

Paul Weyrich

Kevin Phillips

Barbara Walters

Richard Cohen

Al Hunt

David Broder

The New York Review of Books

The New York Times Book Review

That poor man's Walt Kelly, Garry Trudeau

That poor man's Garry Trudeau, Berke Breathed

Herblock

Managua's Herblock, Paul Conrad

New York City Mayor David Dinkins

The National Resource Defense Council

Lawyers Guild
The D.C. Statehood Party
Mayor of Burlington, Vermont, Peter Clavelle
The Berkeley City Council
Berkeley
Mother Jones
The Nation
The Village Voice
Any organization with "Peace" in its name
Donald Trump (OK, so he's not a pinko, but I don't like him. And if
   McCarthyism isn't good for settling grudges, what is it good for?)
The English Department at Duke
The Law School at Harvard
The Liberal Arts Faculty at Stanford
Any educator using the term "Eurocentric" (While we're at it, let's
   reintroduce corporal punishment in the schools—and use it on the
   teachers.)
Salman Rushdie (Kick 'em when they're down is what I say.)
Martin Sheen
Charlie Sheen
*The rest of the Sheen family plus Rob Lowe, Judd Nelson, Demi Moore,
   Molly Ringwald, and all the other Brat Pack members* (Which
   brings to mind another idea for a modified blacklist—this list would
   require left-wingers to write movie scripts, but only for Brat Pack
   movies.)

And let's not forget that most subversive of all organizations in America, the
American government:

Sen. Tom Harkin (D-IA)
Sen. John Kerry (D-MA)
Sen. Barbara Mikulski (D-MD)
Rep. Pete Stark (D-CA)
Rep. Barbara Boxer (D-CA)
Rep. Ed Markey (D-MA)
Rep. Gerry Studds (D-MA)

And from Michigan—an improbable place to find a nest of jacobin no-good-
niks—these Not-the-Reagan-Democrats:

Rep. David Bonior
Rep. John Conyers

And that's just a beginning. Readers of the *American Spectator* were invited to submit their own suggestions—and lots of them. Prepare for a bloodbath—well, a phlegm and bile bath anyway.

Maybe we can reconquer our body politic. Maybe we can sweep the ideologically homeless from the streets of our Shining City on a Hill. Or maybe we can't. It might all backfire the way the splendid fifties backfired and led to the wretched and unspeakable sixties. Still, it's worth a try. At the very least, "Red Scare—The Sequel" will rile the lefties and get them out demonstrating again so policemen can hit them on the head. The police have been having a rough time lately, what with crack and Miranda rights. They need some fun. And one other great good will have been accomplished. We will have found a job for J. Danforth Quayle. He's the perfect point man for Nouvelle McCarthyism, a Senator Joe Lite if ever there was one. Besides, I'm sure he'd much rather have a reputation for evil than the reputation he's got now. ❖

◄ II ►

The
Readers
Respond

The American Spectator, October 1989

I've got a little list—I've got a little list
Of society's offenders who might well be underground,
And who never would be missed—who never would be missed!

. . . the idiot who praises, with enthusiastic tone,
All centuries but this, and every country but his own;

. . . And apologetic statesmen of the compromising kind,
Such as—What-d'ye-call-him—Thing'em-Bob, and likewise—
  Never Mind,
And 'St—'st—'st—and What's-his-name, and also—
  You-know-who—
(The task of filling up the blanks I'd rather leave to you!)
                                                        —W. S. Gilbert

We need some means of persecuting neuterers, nutters, and screaming greenies, some way to abuse entitlement tramps, participants in Gorby orgies, men who think the government is their mother, and women who think government can do the mothering for them. Let's give a wedgie to the whiners, criers, and wet smacks in mortarboards. Let's soap the windows of those who would beggar achievement, vandalize the lawn ornaments of magical thinkers, and heave rotten fruit at haters of beef, gin, and cigars. Let's tell ghost stories to the mollycoddles who fear atomic power, military strength, and the very puissance of Western Civilization itself and turn the garden hose on people who can't bear their freedoms, their selves, or their society and want to vent those pathetic loathings on us, their betters.

Such was my call to action, and the reader response was heartening. Almost a thousand individuals, institutions, and categories of morons were proposed for execration.

THE ENEMIES LIST—THE OVERVIEW

The "New McCarthyism" article was accompanied by a brief muster roll of nitwits—some hundred-odd names with which to chum the waters of indignation. This pilot catalog wasn't meant to be definitive; nonetheless, readers greeted the omission of Teddy Kennedy and Jesse Jackson with howls of indignation. Well, all I can say is, Stalin and Molotov weren't on Senator Joe's original list.

However, neither the Hymietown Rhymer nor In-the-Drink Eddie received the most Enemies List nominations. That distinction belongs, oddly enough, to

Senator Howard Metzenbaum (D-OH). Howie is a terrific fool, of course, and a typical liberal of stinking wealth who's got his pile and would change the rules so nobody else can get theirs. But there are thousands like Howie. Why did almost a quarter of the *American Spectator's* Enemies List respondents mention Metzenbaum by name? Maybe it's because the NRA has been targeting the Buckeye Bolshie for his disarm-the-populace legislative proposals. (The events in Tiananmen Square have given liberals new impetus on this issue—just think how many People's Army soldiers might have been killed if China didn't have the benefit of gun control.) Let that *American Spectator*-NRA overlap be fair warning to the pink-squeeks. Not only do we conservatives support the Second Amendment, we also exercise our Second Amendment rights. We've got a bunch of guns, and all you liberals have is Carl Rowan, who had a trophy-size stoned teenager trapped in his own backyard and couldn't manage a kill shot.

Also surprisingly popular as objects of derision were Linda Ellerbee, Leonard Bernstein, and Ramsey Clark—not exactly America's major trio of power-brokering opinion-molders, if you ask me. But annoyance factor seemed to outweigh public danger in readers' minds. Carl Sagan, Whoopi Goldberg, Mitch Snyder, and C. Everett Koop (that buttinski) each collected a larger number of blackballs than did the ACLU. And Barney Frank was damned with greater frequency than Christopher Dodd or Louis Farrakhan.

More predictably, there was plenty of media-baiting—of Dan Rather and Sam Donaldson in particular and of National Public Radio in general. Ted Turner was repeatedly condemned as a traitor, though not (let free enterprise reign) as a colorist.

Other multiple citations: Al Sharpton, despised as a demagogue. Mike Dukakis, despised as a loser. Molly Yard, despised period (pun semi-intended).

One problem mooted in the original article was inventing a modern punishment to go with a modern McCarthyism. Our jails are too full already. And why should we impose the likes of Howard Metzenbaum on ordinary, decent crack dealers? I had proposed media overexposure as a form of revenge—putting our victims in supermarket tabloids and on television talk shows until the public gagged and condemned them to remote dinner theater productions. But now I'm not so sure. That is, media overexposure worked like a charm on Morton Downey, Jr., but has failed to make the slightest dent in Rob Lowe. (And how much more overexposed can you get?) In this matter the readers were no help at all. In fact, the faint sound of tumbrels rolling can be heard in the background of more than a few Enemies List missives. Hey, dudes, lighten up.

While I'm on the tactless tack of criticizing the paying customers, let me say you folks are a bit rough with black leaders. Sure, they spout nonsense but it's in the great nonsense-spouting tradition of Irish, Italians, and Jews before them.

This is the way poor people acquire job skills. How can blacks climb the American socioeconomic ladder and get big jobs in industry and government if they don't know how to be as completely full of crap as the rest of us? A bit of invert-bashing was also detectable in some letters. Now, whatever we (and God) may think about this method of birth control, let us not forget that at the core of conservatism is the sanctity of the individual and the privacy of the conscience. Also, if you think there's no such thing as an influential gay conservative, you sure haven't been reading the *Washington Times* lately.

That said, the following register of enemies, including reader comments, is presented in the order received and edited only to eliminate repetition. (I've made my own addenda when I thought the correspondent was seriously receiving radio messages from Neptune on his dentures.) Every nomination has been included no matter how wacky, obscure, imaginary, or dead the choice. There are only three exceptions.

1. Arnold Schwarzenegger. Someone actually proposed Arnold Schwarzenegger for the New Enemies List, and I'm going to save that person's life. Besides, Arnold is a big-time Republican and watching him marry into the Kennedy clan was one of the most satisfying spectacles of the late twentieth century. Here's this family of bigmouths who pride themselves on being rough and tough and suddenly they have a mossback in-law who can snap all their spines with the muscles in his smaller toes.

2. Mike Royko. Somebody suggested him, too, but I'm not having it. In the first place, Mike is one of the last newspapermen on earth who still hang out in bars instead of computer stores or leg-waxing salons. In the second place, he wrote a column a couple of months ago in which he wondered where all the bums, soaks, and rummies had gone and then realized they'd all become members of advocacy groups and were demonstrating outside the White House. In the third place, Mike's got a tongue like a lash and I don't want to be in its way.

3. Pat Schroeder. Pat was nominated for the List almost as many times as Molly Yard, but what use is perpetrating arbitrary injustice if I can't be arbitrary about it? I don't agree with the Honorable Ms. Schroeder about much, but I like her. She says what she thinks and adds a much-needed lightness of tone to the dreadful House of Representatives. And, as for Pat weeping during her presidential campaign, hell, all I had to do was watch the '88 election on TV and I howled like a tyke in a month-old Pamper.

One more omission: Representative Mickey Leland (D-TX) died in a plane crash in Ethiopia. Congressman Leland was named by a number of readers, but common decency demands that we forgo his inclusion. Instead, we'll include his staff. Leland's aides bitched loudly about the "inadequate" efforts to find their boss. The Pentagon deployed one C-5 cargo plane, three C-141 cargo planes, four C-130 search-and-rescue planes, four UH-60 helicopters, a weather satellite, and a U-2 spy plane in the hunt for Leland. Usually when this kind of taxpayer money is spent on a Texas congressman, it's for purposes of prosecution.

THE LIST ITSELF

But before we begin the actual list, let's hear from a couple of people who eschewed naming names and took broad philosophical views instead.

One Keith Roberts suggests that:

> Before we exorcise the left, let's straighten out our own ranks. . . .With Reagan came fellow travelers from the left—Reagan Democrats and religious Nazis and kinder, gentler Welfare State Conservatives.
> Sure, crush the lefties, but save some ideological muscle for the brown shirts and hairshirts of the right: wannabe bureaucrat businessmen and Bible-toting bomb-heaving Christians.

Thank you for sharing, Keith, and keep your head down.

John Poulin of Flin Flon, Manitoba, worries about the effect our housecleaning may have on his large, wishy-washy nation:

> Usually I leave American issues to Americans, but the repercussions of Tail-Gunnerism redux are bound to spill over into this benighted land. . . . Large numbers of sensitive citizens here were traumatized by the fear-crazed thousands who tumbled northward during the last purge and began drinking heavily, thus making the roads hazardous.

Mr. Poulin gives some sage advice to fugitives from political ridicule: "All expatriots and expelled rabble who drift northward should dress warmly, as winters here are coldish. . . . Most of our politicians are either lunatics or scoundrels. . . . Chances are good that your riffraff can get good jobs working for the government."

Finally, there was a solitary letter of dissent. Phil Maggitti of Elverson, Pennsylvania, wrote: "In the midst of an otherwise admirable and occasionally funny piece in your July issue, P. J. 'He's No Tom Wolfe' O'Rourke takes the obligatory cheap shot at animal rights activists . . ." Phil had a lot more to say but a bear ate him.

Now, the list.

Thomas J. Bieter of Duluth, Minnesota, kicks off with:

> *Minnesota State Rep. Phyllis Kahn,* who introduced a bill which would have granted the vote to twelve-year-olds. She was serious. Arguments against her bill, she charged, display an "adult supremacist attitude."

Robert W. Somers of Carrboro, North Carolina, names:

> *The Raleigh News and Observer:* This birdcage liner has kept the ravings of Cockburn, McGrory, and Lewis while purging the writings of R. E. Tyrrell and Joe Bob Briggs.

They pulled Joe Bob Briggs? We *are* aghast.

Nicholas A. Damask II of Cincinnati, Ohio, who signs himself "an obviously racist-sexist-fascist-homophobic college student," suggests:

> *Sen. Christopher "Nicaraguan Foreign Minister" Dodd* (D-CT)
> *Rep. Henry B. Gonzalez* (D-TX)
> *Whoopi Goldberg*
> *Robin "Wish I Were Whoopi Goldberg" Williams*
> *Don Johnson*
> *Barbra Streisand*
> *David Corn*
> *Robert Scheer*
> *Mark Green*
> *Lesley Stahl*
> *Katharine Graham*
> *All college presidents except John Silber and George Roche*

"Shocked to find the following names missing from the New Enemies List," says Lawrence D. Skutch of Westport, Connecticut:

> *John Dingell* (D-MI), whose recent pronouncements on scientific method make this country appear "a buffoon among great nations"
> *Bill Bradley* (D-NJ), who pulled strings to join a reserve unit during Vietnam so he could continue his important work—playing basketball
> *Sam Nunn* (D-GA), whose only useful action is to prove a chairman of the Senate Foreign Relations Committee is unfit to be secretary of defense

Johnny Carson, whose only funny line in almost thirty years was that Jim Wright would resign as Speaker as soon as he could find a buyer for the office

Jay Leno, who thinks the mere mention of J. Danforth Quayle should regale the assorted hinds with laughter

Edward Kennedy (D-MA), who, while enjoying the fruits of a $400 million trust fund, can't spend the rest of the country's money fast enough

James A. Morgan of Martinsburg, West Virginia, proposes:
Jane Fonda
Molly Yard
Barbara Ehrenreich
Kate Michelman
And my peacenik friends George and Linda from Pittsburgh, whom I suspect would secretly *love* to be on a right-wing enemies list

Terry Przybylski of Des Plaines, Illinois, says of his dishonor roll, "This is all I have time for right now. I must return to witch-hunting, Commie-bashing, and improving my techniques for gambling at bowling":
Jesse Jackson, his wife, his kids, his neighbors, anyone who ever voted for him and anyone who ever trained a camera on him
Lyndon LaRouche, so the lefties in the media will quit calling him an "arch-conservative"
Bella Abzug
USA Today
Vernon Jarrett, race-baiting columnist for the *Chicago Sun-Times*
The "Tempo Woman" section of the Chicago Tribune, presented every Sunday by the Women's International Conspiracy from Hell
Betty Friedan
Kate Millet
Susan Brownmiller
Margaret Atwood
Cardinal Bernardin of Chicago
Archbishop Weakland of Milwaukee
Any priest, minister, or rabbi who was in the seminary or divinity school during the Vietnam War, to be defrocked by one of his peers who was there
NAACP
ADA
ACLU

UAW: Sorry, *American Spectator,* sometimes you have to offend your
  advertisers.
Ann Arbor, Michigan
Madison, Wisconsin
Iowa City, Iowa
Marvin Miller, the former head of the baseball players union, for
  calling American academia a "right-wing" institution

Bryan R. Johnson of Blacksburg, Virginia, says, "If it is later discovered that an innocent person has been placed on the list, we can do what the Soviets do—rehabilitate their names about fifty years after they're dead." And he nominates:
The American Library Association
Jack Anderson
Handgun Control, Inc.
Carl Rowan, Jr.
*The entire cast, producers, writers, and, what the hell, even the
  cameramen of the* Today Show: Let's bring back the concept of "guilt
  by association."

Bill Wiltman of Dade City, Florida, submits:
Anybody who thinks Mahler was a great composer
The progeny of Henry Ford and R. J. Reynolds
Howard Cosell
"Also," says Bill, "I suggest developing a schedule of traits common to all members of the List. For example, going 'Humph!' and rolling the eyes when someone mentions Nixon. Or saying 'Oh, God!' at the mention of Reagan. Or clapping at movies, considering the dead ducks in Alaska 'a crime against humanity,' and saying 'Oh, God! You read *that?*' about the *American Spectator.* Such a list is needed because we are all susceptible to frauds now and then, even the best fraud detectives. Mencken voted for Roosevelt in '32."

"The following," writes Robert Y. Stair of Ocala, Florida, "are creatures who display no redeeming characteristics":
Daniel Schorr
Ramsey Clark
Stansfield Turner
Ernest Hollings
Tom Brokaw
Redneck TV evangelists

The Department of Education
All the Pentagon desk jockeys who collected medals for the Grenada
*   invasion but never left town*

Comes now Mary Frances Vollmer of Colorado Springs, Colorado, whose enemies include a number of my friends and acquaintances, starting with Pat Schroeder, who, as I mentioned, will not be mentioned. Here, however, is the rest of the Vollmer Index:

Sen. Alan Cranston (D-CA)
Eleanor Holmes Norton
Garrick Utley
Jack Germond
Haynes Johnson
Michael Kinsley
Chris Matthews
Eleanor Clift
Michael Jackson, the radio talk show host, not the singer
Steve Roberts (*New York Times*)
Chris Wallace
Mark Shields
Tom Braden
Jack Nelson (*Los Angeles Times*)

Let me beg to differ on Garrick Utley, Mary Frances. He's always been good about plugging my books, and there are some things more important than politics—car payments, just for instance. Michael Kinsley—a close friend of mine and a dear enemy of R. Emmett's—is liberalish, true, but the thing he likes best about liberalism is being accused of it. Then there's Chris Matthews. What can I say, Chris? I'll try to make sure you're well treated in detention.

William Milton Macfadyen of Santa Barbara, California, sends us a neatly typed, inclusive, and alphabetized syllabus. He's obviously been keeping a file on these people. Stick around, Mac, we're going to need you during the Quayle administration:

ABA
The Hon. James A. Baker III
The Rev. Jim Bakker
Bob Beckel
The Hon. Joe Biden
The Miserable Jack Brooks
The Hon. Willie Brown
California's Democratic congressional delegation

The Dishonorable Tony Coelho
EarthFirst! PeopleLast?
Michael G. Gartner
Jessica Hahn
The Hon. Lee H. Hamilton
Gary Hartpence or Gephardt or whatever his name is
Stephen Hess
Joan Kroc
Spuds MacKenzie
MADD
Ralph Neas
The New York Times
Timesmen and Timeswomen Linda Greenhouse, Lindsey Gruson, Stephen
    Kinzer, and Robin Toner
Planned Parenthood
Harvey Rosenfield
Eleanor Smeal
Mitch Snyder
The Hon. Arlen Specter
David Stockman
Robert Strauss
Laurence Tribe
The Unitarian Society
West Germany: Don't they ever learn?
Brian "Shorty" Willson

   John F. Curran of River Edge, New Jersey, gives us the following excellent
suggestions:
   Little kids who become pen pals of totalitarians and the media who suck
       this stuff up
   Jim Wright, who did not so much resign from Congress as permit
       Congress to withdraw from him
   Sweden
   Pete Hamill, for finding a parallel between the Chicago '68 punks and the
       students in Tiananmen Square
   Anyone who refers to the handicapped as "differently abled": I suppose
       the dead are "differently vital."
   Richard Serra and his annoyingly intrusive Tilted Arc *sculpture*
   The ideologically correct pronunciation masters: "Nicaragua," in English,
       is "knicker-rog-wa." And what's this "Chee-lay" stuff? I wonder how
       these people pronounce "France"?

Geraldine Ferraro and family
All bemoaners of "insensitivity"
All "nuclear-free zones"
The perpetrators of the hyphenated last name syndrome
Feminists who insist upon ragging patriarchy by retaining, upon
marriage, their daddies' names
J. F. Kennedy, Jr.
Lawyers: The Antichrist will have a law degree, of this I am certain.

Tom Lauria of Arlington, Virginia, notes that our first chapter "overlooked some major, A-list comsymp redheads. But, hey," he continues, "now that the Right has its own 'Names Project'. . .":
Those scarlet-beaked birdbrains at National Public Radio, especially the
staff of All Things Considered
Cat Stevens
Darryl Hannah
Bob Barker
Flora Lewis
Joan Baez
And that true red tool, City Paper *editor Jack Shafer*
Just a minute here, Tom, Jack Shafer isn't a "red tool," he's a Libertarian—similar to a conservative except he believes we should all have private Polaris missiles in our backyard pools. As for Darryl Hannah, you may be right about her politics, but I'm sure somebody can talk some sense into her. I volunteer.

James J. Griffitts of Dunnellon, Florida, protests my plan for media overexposure. He thinks some people should be banned from television entirely:
Old Nixon, Johnson, and Carter experts who hover in covens along the
Potomac
Robert McNamara
CIA's Colby: an obvious security risk
Griffitts also suggests that subcommittees made up of blacks, Episcopalians, Jews, journalists, and Republicans should be set up to select numbers of their own to be banished from the media, e.g.:
Andrew Young
Barbara Jordan
Desmond Tutu
Headman Browning
Alan Dershowitz
Charlayne Hunter-Gault

> *Paul Sarbanes*
> *And maybe Richard Nixon*

Richard Nixon? You've gone too far, James. We'll have to make one more addition to the Enemies List here and now:

> *James J. Griffitts*

Marion E. Mahony of Roanoke, Virginia, forwards a list "compiled with much phlegm, bile, and—and barf!!!":

> *Ex-Gov. Douglas Wilder of Virginia*
> *Ex-Gov. Mario Cuomo of New York*
> *Sen. Chuck Robb of Virginia*
> *Ex-Sen. Paul Trible* (R-VA), quitter and turncoat!
> *Numerous Roman Catholic bishops, clergy, and dissident nuns: I* am a
>   Roman Catholic—but am no leftist or libertarian
> *Columnist William Raspberry,* an ordinarily sensible man who supports
>   Jesse Jackson for PRESIDENT!!!
> *Louis Farrakhan*
> *Paxton Davis,* a radical leftist columnist in our local paper
> *PLOWSHARES*
> *Armand Hammer*
> *Gloria Steinem*
> *Larry Flynt*
> *Hugh and Christie Hefner*
> *Paul Newman:* He's beautiful and talented and I love him—but I HATE
>   HIS POLITICS!!!

Well put, Marion, but Gloria Steinem is from my hometown of Toledo, Ohio, and, believe me, she's got a reason to be crazy.

Jeff Kock and Ken Pitts of Nashville, Tennessee, say:

> *Mary McGrory*

and add, "We propose legislation mandating that all newspapers carrying both 'Doonesbury' and Miss McGrory's column drop 'Doonesbury' and put Mary's dribble on the comics page."

Marjorie G. James of Austin, Texas, tells us, "I get a lot of mail from celebrities, and they want to hear from me, too. In fact they even send me addressed envelopes and sometimes postage. So—please":

> *Joanne Woodward,* who wants to keep back-alley abortionists at bay
> *Jimmy Carter,* who wants to keep on hammering
> *Lily Tomlin,* who helped to make Ann Richards governor of Texas

Ann Richards
Ann Lewis
Plus:
Massachusetts
New York City
Dan Rather
Walter Cronkite
Cathy Cronkite: Walter's daughter who has a radio talk show here and gets
   downright testy with callers who show just a speck of good sense

   Dr. Alfred M. Beyer of Garden City, New York, would like to add:
   National Geographic
"This may raise some eyebrows," says Dr. Al, "but I have long considered it a
left-leaning mag. Every two or three months they show us a 'People's Republic'
country with smiling peasants and citizens."

S teve J. Adamek of San Diego, California, calls us timid. "The nation re-
quires a complete perestroika," he claims. "We must say *bon voyage* to":
   Ex–gang members and ex–drug addicts who have become drug
       counselors and youth activists
"This will open the job market for current addicts and gang members. Thus we
will be left with only one problem, the sagging domestic assault rifle industry.
This can be solved by the time-honored trade practice of government-subsidized
dumping. The outskirts of Nicaragua and the interior of China seem good places
to test this policy."

   Mark Sheffield, Jr., of Escondido, California, decries:
   Paul Duke
   Frederick Allen
   Cokie Roberts
   Judy Woodruff
   Cher
   Sally Quinn
   William Hurt
   Maxine Waters
   MacNeil-Lehrer and Company
   Rep. Henry Waxman (D-CA)

   Dave Wilson of Denver, Colorado, recommends for animadversion:

Helen Caldicott

Sam Donaldson

John Chancellor: He actually suggested in a commentary that the U.S.
government subsidize an American book tour by Salman Rushdie.

The Massachusetts congressional delegation: Send in the clowns.

Rep. James Traficant, Jr. (D-OH)

Actor John Cusack: He claims that because of his anti-Reagan statements,
a government agent is probably monitoring his phone calls—talk about
a lousy civil service job.

Elayne Boosler: the comedy club answer to Mme. Defarge, although
Defarge was better at keeping people in stitches

Dayton, Ohio: Hometown of the acting Lowe brothers, Rob and Chad.
What a comedown from being the hometown of the flying Wright
brothers, Orville and Wilbur.

Larry King: He hangs up on callers who disagree with him within eight
seconds.

Callers who agree with Larry King: He hangs up on them within twelve
seconds.

Personally, Dave, I think Larry King redeems himself for the former by the lat-
ter. Besides, he once gave me an even better book plug than Garrick Utley.

James R. Stevenson, address unknown, reproves:

George Steinbrenner: Anyone who can destroy baseball so thoroughly
has got to be a pinko.

C. Everett Koop

E.T.: Is anybody on this list truly human?

The American Roman Catholic Bishops: Heretics all!

David Rockefeller: Hey, this is an enemies list! It has to have a
Rockefeller. Otherwise, we'll give paranoia a bad name.

And James signs his letter with a rather strict "OFF THE PINKS!" ❖

◄ III ►

The Readers Keep Responding

springs

Those of you who took President Bush's "kinder, gentler" suggestion too literally and, therefore, haven't been reading the *American Spectator* may wonder what's going on here. Well, in the July 1989 issue I first proposed a "New McCarthyism" (of the Strike-a-Blow-for-Joe, not the Clean-for-Gene type). This would be fair recompense to the left, I thought, for their incessant use of the Mc-word to describe every conservative criticism of anybody.

At the end of my "Proscription for a Better America" I asked readers to send in the names of additional goats to scape. Send they did—postcards, letters, telegrams, and computer printouts thick as a Democrat's skull. This despite the fact that *American Spectator* readers have jobs, marriages, intellects, and other things which keep them busier than, say, members of the Community for Creative Nonviolence. So many parlor pinks, bull slingers, dweebs, wonks, bluestockings, nincompoops, hopheads, muck spouts, hog callers, dopes, simps, chumps, wets, sob sisters, egg suckers, and pencil-necked geeks were named that the Readers' List had to be divided into two parts.

We now have a lovely file on the ideologically sinister, a fine, big matricula of scum. The only problem is, no one has come up with a fit suggestion for what to do with the people on it. We conservatives don't have gulags because they aren't tax deductible. You can't leverage gulag assets, and gulag merchandising rights are worth zilch. I mean, who wants a Leonid Brezhnev lunch box? Drug therapy isn't going to work on these folks. Most of the lefties already tried it on themselves in the sixties. And prefrontal lobotomies are out. How can doctors sever the nerves connecting the frontal lobes with the thalamus when the entire brain is absent? Maybe we can crate up the nitwits and sell them in Eastern Europe. I hear they're running out of Commies over there.

THE LIST CONTINUES

Anyway, as I have noted, the Readers' Enemies List has been edited only to remove duplications, and the comments appearing after the italicized names are the readers' own, although there is an occasional bracketed note from me when I thought somebody was calling in an air strike on his own position.

Paul J. Beck of Morocco, Indiana, begins the back nine play, teeing off on:
Studs Terkel
Joseph Campbell
Forrest Church
Sondra Gehr, local Chicago public radio host, a feminine Terkel

Presidents of Dartmouth and Stanford
Maureen Reagan, who gives freeloading off a famous father a bad name
Mortimer Adler
Little Stevie
David Lange
The ACLU attorneys who tried to send Walter Polovchak to the gulag
That rheumy-eyed guy from Harvard who writes those weepy books about children. Whatsisname.
Richard Lamm: This man is scary.

Judith Evans Hanhisalo of Duxbury, Massachusetts, wants to add to the list:
Lawrence Walsh and his entire secret police organization
Judge Gerhard Gesell
Adm. Gene La Rocque
But she wants to subtract from our previous list:
Paul Weyrich
Not until he buys John Tower a drink.

William Rockwood of Canoga Park, California, reproaches:
Michael J. Fox and the entire cast of Family Ties
Rosanna Arquette
Marlon Brando
The makers of nonalcoholic wine

"I've tried," says Doug Rivers of Warner Robbins, Georgia, "to group my candidates for the New Enemies List by certain common characteristics to facilitate future classification at re-education camps":
Alice Walker: All on the final list should be forced to read one of her novels cover to cover.
Mick and Bianca Jagger
Gregory Peck
The ol' Cos, Tawana Brawley patron
Gene Upshaw
Right Reverend Sharpton
Attorneys Mason and Maddox
Presbyterians
Vegetarians
Presbyterians?

Kenneth M. Potter of Pittsburgh, Pennsylvania, indicts the following:

Paul Warnke
Sen. Patrick "Leaker" Leahy
"Preacher" Scotty Reston

Sammy Thompson III of Washington, D.C., writes on behalf of himself and his associates to say, "As junior staff peons at two neoconservative organizations, we join together to form the Mortals & Divine Society, whose mission is to take every occasion to publicly and privately denounce and harangue those listed below":

Elizabeth Drew
Jane Pauley
Sojourners *magazine*
Jim Wallis
John Lofton
The Other Side *magazine*
John Keker
Bishop John Shelby Spong
I. F. Stone, also on God's list
Gus Hall
Timothy Leary
Jim Hightower
Pat Sajak
Morton Downey, Jr.
John Nields
Arthur Liman
Gloria Allred
David Duke
Buz Lukens
The Kennedy Kids
Larry "Bud" Melman
Mayor Marion Barry
Leonard Nimoy
The Fairfax County "Family Life Education" program
People who use "dove" motifs
Dykes on Bikes
Eugene McCarthy
TransAfrica
The Hollywood Women's Political Committee
The inventor of the "Visualize World Peace" bumper sticker

Joseph J. Eule, also of D.C., admonishes:
Arthur Schlesinger, Jr.

A. Bartlett Giamatti: A liberal as commissioner of baseball? Something pretty fishy there if you ask me. [Obviously the Big Umpire upstairs agreed.]
Rep. Sam Gejdenson
Anybody using the term "significant other"
All Yugo owners
Smith College School for Social Work

Peter Cuikas of Leominster, Massachusetts, proscribes:
Mike Dukakis
Boston Globe *editorial page contributor David Nyhan*
Rep. Barney Frank (D-MA)
The Clamshell Alliance
Jeremy Rifkin
Sally Struthers
Bill Moyers
And my brother-in-law, who is living testimony to the meaninglessness of a college degree these days

Paul Kirchner of Hamden, Connecticut, reviles:
Oliver Stone
Linda "Is anyone going to eat that last éclair?" Ellerbee
Charles Kuralt
Paul Simon: both of them
Lillian Hellman: deceased but in need of further persecution
Paul Robeson: ditto
Norman Mailer
Kurt Vonnegut
William Styron, and anyone else who would describe Mr. and Mrs. Ortega as "poets"
Anyone who uses the terms "The Third World" and "The Homeless" respectfully
Jon Voight
Everyone who sang on "We Are the World," especially that turncoat redneck Willie Nelson
Ad agency people who write jingles for giant corporations that sound like additional stanzas to "We Are the World"
Rep. Robert Torricelli
Rep. Joe Kennedy, Jr., and every other Kennedy except maybe Caroline
Bob Geldof
David Byrne

Rock groups that take up left-wing politics under the mistaken idea that they have something to contribute to society besides a driving backbeat and three-chord progressions
Jack Lemmon
Morgan Fairchild
Actresses who take up left-wing politics under the mistaken idea that they have something to contribute to society besides a good look at their breasts
Dick Gregory
Philip Agee
Randall Robinson
Susan Stamberg
Nina Totenberg
Linda Wertheimer
Anyone who held a candle for Ted Bundy
Ben Bradlee
Bob "He sat up in his bed! He talked to me! I swear it!" Woodward
Garry Wills
Peter Ustinov
Pete Seeger
Arlo Guthrie
Folksingers
Poets
Mimes
Sydney Schanberg, wherever he is
Frank Zappa, former iconoclast, now boring knee-jerk liberal
Hunter Thompson, ditto
William Greider

Paul, I don't mind your putting my friend and co-worker William Greider on the list, because he'd be darned upset if he were left off. But you'd better watch what you say about my pal Hunter or the next time you visit your stamp collection you may find the back of your Eisenhower memorial block has been dosed with Ibogaine.

To return to our sheep, Mary and Timothy Wheeler of Shelbyville, Indiana, fulminate at length, and somewhat peevishly, thus:
Ernest Sternglass
Amory Lovins
Barry Commoner
Andrew Greeley

E. F. Schumacher
Sidney Blumenthal
Richard J. Barnet
Madalyn Murray O'Hair
Irving Howe
Robert Drinan
Norman Birnbaum
Madonna
Maria Shriver
Michael Gartner, editor of the Ames, Iowa, *Daily Tribune*
Eddie Murphy
Janet Cooke
One Mary Farley, who described "My Love Affair with a Sandinista" in
    Cosmo. Lust on a park bench, actually.
Cybill Shepherd
Msgr. Bryan Hehir
Sid and Nancy
Jack Valenti
Dr. Ruth
Kathleen Sullivan
Jean Harris
Guns N' Roses
Betty Dodson
James Freedman
William Cole
Joyce Carol Oates
Tony Mandarich
Mike Tyson [Okay, Mary and Tim, howsabout *you* go tell Mike he's on
    the Enemies List.]
Robin Givens
Irving R. Levine
Ted Sorensen
Bob Rafelson
Alex Cox
Arthur Penn
John Denver
Richard Pryor
Judy Collins
Charles Curran
Barry Manilow

Jack Henry Abbott
Glenn Close
Safe sex
Chuck Stone
Kim Basinger
Dustin Hoffman
Sushi
Willie Horton
Candy Crowley
Carroll O'Connor
Jack Klugman
Alice Rivlin
Muzak
Harold Stassen
Mary Worth
Martin Scorsese
Candice Bergen
#12 grade river gravel [huh?]
Gallaudet College
Union of Concerned Alchemists
Scientific American
Oregon
West 57th Street
The U.S. House of Representatives
*Everyone in the Senate whose weight exceeds his IQ by a factor of two or
    more:* Attn: Ted
Anybody on Saturday Night Live
Any given Supreme Court majority or minority
Feminists in slacks
Ugly feminists
Old feminists
Ecofeminists
Feminist dykes
Masculine feminists
Anyone who uses "Ms." without wincing
Social workers
Pollsters
Therapists
Bureaucrats
Activists

Slugs

Anyone who believes in homophobia

Anyone who disapproves of it

Everyone at every prestige university except first-semester freshmen, maybe

Anyone who consciously forms "relationships"

*Anyone belonging to any group that has "Coalition," "Alliance,"
"Community," "Solidarity," "Citizen," "People," or "Popular" in
its name*

*Anyone who refers to "the movement" and is not talking about bodily
functions*

*Anyone who observes, studies, analyzes, or dithers on about race, class,
and gender*

And a special He-Has-Grown Prize to Mikhail Gorbachev

Whew. You two don't fool around, do you?

"**I** am a Catholic priest: usually good-natured, and occasionally utterly exasperated," writes the Reverend Dennis P. Lyden of Bellaire, Ohio. Herewith his causes of utter exasperation:

The San Francisco Board of Supervisors

Writers, producers, and cast of Fox's 21 Jump Street *and, come to
think of it, the whole Fox operation*

Kurt Loder of MTV News

MTV

Writers, producers, and cast of ABC's Head of the Class

Jerry Jones, owner of the Dallas Cowboys

Richard Gere

Siskel and Ebert

Sir Richard Attenborough

NAMBLA

Pittsburgh and Atlanta police departments

Burt Lancaster

Thomas Stoddard

Producers of Folgers coffee commercials

Writers, producers, and cast of CBS's Kate & Allie

Anyone yammering on about the "spirit of Vatican II"

Liturgical commissions

Peace and Justice offices

Prince

WOC (Women's Ordination Conference)

Garfield

German, Dutch, and Belgian theologians
Expurgators of "sexist" language in divine worship
The administration of Georgetown University

An anonymous correspondent from Eugene, Oregon, blacklists:
Dwight Eisenhower: emeritus distinction
Eleanor Roosevelt: ditto
Jack Odell, Jesse Jackson's foreign policy advisor who's so Stalinist he
    couldn't win an election in the Soviet Union
Mary Hatwood Futrell
Marian Wright Edelman: While we're at it, anyone who uses three names
    merits further investigation.
The National Civil Liberties Emergency Committee
Victor Rabinowitz of same
The sanctuary movement and its organ Basta!
The Chicago Religious Task Force on Central America
Its leaders, Renny Golden and Michael McConnell
Prairie Fire
Franklin Thomas, president of the Ford Foundation
The Ford Foundation: Back in the original McCarthy days, the John
    Birch Society was wackily obsessed by the Ford Foundation, but since
    then the Foundation has grown into the job.

 Jonathan J. Cohen, living in the very belly of the beast in Brookline, Massachusetts, lashes out against:
Marty Nolan
Ellen Goodman
Thomas Oliphant
Charles Pierce, gonzo-radical sportswriter for the *Boston Herald*
Rep. Charles Rangel (D-NY)
Ron Brown
Witt-Thomas-Harris Productions (*Golden Girls, Soap,* etc.)
Crosby, Stills, and Nash: Spare Neil Young because he's Canadian
People for the American Way
The movie Old Gringo: Based on a Carlos Fuentes novel, with Jane Fonda
    and Gregory Peck—to die for, right?
Woody Allen
Rita Hauser
The EPA
Stanley Sheinbaum
Anyone who signed those pro-Palestinian ads in the New York Times

Lars-Erik Nelson and Jack Newfield of the New York Daily News:
    Would you believe it? Archie Bunker's old paper has gone lefty.

John S. Davidge of Binghamton, New York, denounces:
Jessica Lange
Robert Heilbroner
Richard Goodwin
Burke Marshall
Henry Commager
Cornell's Department of African Studies
The New Yorker
Time
Newsweek
Rudolph Giuliani
Richard Reeves
Jimmy Breslin
John Gofman
Tim Wirth
George McGovern
Charles Schumer
John Heinz
Augustus Hawkins
Susan Estrich
Les Aspin
Robert Byrd
Aryeh Neier
John K. Galbraith
James K. Galbraith
Henry L. Gates
Bishop Paul Moore
Peter Bradford
Leonard Sand
Sierra Club
Friends of the Earth
Lee Iacocca
Frances Piven
Clyde Prestowitz
Jeff Faux
Robert Reich
Kronos Quartet

Ali Mazrui
Kathy Boudin
Bernadine Dohrn
Larry Davis
Susan Tipograph
Clarence Ditlow
Joan Claybrook
Russell Means
Americas Watch
The United Nations
The World Bank

Richard Bertovich of Eastlake, Ohio, is unhappy with:
Ex.-Gov. Dick Celeste of Ohio
Any politician who uses the term "Economic Justice"
Debra Winger
Hendrik Hertzberg
Sorry that Richard feels this way, Rick, but you *did* go to work in the Carter White House.

Keith J. Yoder of Meyersdale, Pennsylvania, castigates the following with a quote from musician Steve Taylor: "They're so open-minded that their brains leaked out":
Sinead O'Connor
Edie Brickell: would enjoy pushing her into deep water
Peter Gabriel
White Lion
Megadeth
Beach Boys: Reagan can be wrong.
Cyril Scott
The Grammy Awards ceremony
Robert Schuller
Ronald Sider
Faye Wentworth
Ron Reagan, Jr.
Environmental Media Associates
Better World Society
New Group of World Servers
Zero Population Growth
The Congressional Black Caucus

William C. Rice of Ann Arbor, Michigan, reviles:
  Capitol Steps
  Dr. Science
  Educational Testing Service
  Modern Language Association
  October *magazine*

Warren Klofkorn of Manchester, Michigan, vilifies:
  The Consumer Product Safety Commission
  Marian Faupel, my ex-wife's lawyer
  Pete Rose
  United Coalition Against Racism
  Ronald McDonald
  George Bush, for knuckling under to the anti-gun lobby
  Latter-day hippies
  The DEA
And he finishes his list with this doozy—hold the calls, folks, we have a winner:
  Ann Arbor's People's Communist Lesbian Food Co-op

Keith N. Dickey of Forest Hills, Maryland, censures:
  Sen. Claiborne Pell
  Rep. Steny Hoyer (D-MD)
  Any organization that has "freeze" or "nuclear" in its title
  SANE
  "Race Horse" Haynes
  Melvin Belli

Suzy Pollok of Houston, Texas, pleads inclusion of:
  The National Gay and Lesbian Task Force

George M. Mellinger who refers to himself as a resident of "Minneapolis, People's Republic of Minnesota," rails against:
  Everyone named Fonda
  Anyone whose name is even similar to Fonda: With that family we can't
    take any chances. Let God sort 'em out.
  The Mondale family
  Bob Dylan
  Joe Piscopo
  Neil Young: Canadian cultural imperialism!
  Mary Berry

Ellerbee wannabe Andrea Mitchell
Any Union of Concerned anybodies
Any organization that is a "Friends of . . ."
Nikolai Bukharin Fan Club President Stephen F. Cohen

Al Warmington of Cleveland, Ohio, upbraids:
The entire 185,000 members of the IRS
Adlai Stevenson III
Leon Trotsky: Dead, 1940, but we need the hatchet back, given our
    Defense Department's dearth of Truly Threatening Anti-Marxist
    Death Machines

Jason Levine, a lonely and beleaguered conservative student at Brandeis, a
branch campus of Patrice Lumumba University, gets a little of his own back at:
Lynn Samuels, New York City radio talk show hostess with the voice and
    sophistication of that city's cab drivers
Willard Scott: Don't fat, bald men who get rated in the "Ten Most Sexy"
    surveys bug you too? [No, Jason, at age forty-two, the idea of bald, fat,
    and sexy does *not* bother me. And as long as Willard bugs Bryant
    Gumbel, he's OK by me.]
Amnesty International
Jon Bon Jovi
That poor man's Berke Breathed, Doug Marlette
The Whole Earth Catalog
Oprah Winfrey, who could slim down even more if she would refrain
    from putting her foot in her mouth
The Revolutionary Communist Youth Brigade
Gregory "I am not an American" Johnson, their stooge
Rolling Stone (Sorry, P.J.!)
Apology accepted, Jason. But, if I'm fired, can I crash at the dorm for a while?

Joe Skilton of Portland, Oregon, reprehends:
Jerry Brown
Gerald "Jimmy and I are here to help" Ford

A Chicago informant who shall remain nameless would ostracize:
Ira Glasser
Lou Palmer, columnist for the *Chicago Defender*
The Chicago Defender
ACT UP

The Windy City Times, *a gay Chicago newspaper*
ANC
The Liguorian
Planetary Initiative for the World
We Choose, a New Age organization for world unity
The Club of Rome
All adherents of Harmonic Convergence
The Institute for Critical Legal Studies at Harvard Law School
Tom Wicker
Political Science and Sociology Departments at the University of
    Wisconsin
ABC, NBC, and CBS
Vladimir Posner
The Humanist
Robert Sherman, head of the Illinois chapter of the American Atheists'
    Society
Deng Xiaoping
FAIR (Fairness and Accuracy in Reporting)
Harnet Pilpel
Anyone who uses the phrase "chilling effect"
Bob Guccione
The Washington Post
The Advocate
U.S. District Court Judge Eugene Sand (re: alleged housing discrimination
    in New York)
Former Senator William Proxmire
CPUSA (Communist Party, USA)
Communist Socialist Workers' Party
The People's Daily World
Hollywood, California
The National Abortion Rights Action League
Operation PUSH
The Hemlock Society
Dred Scott Tyler, of flag-treading fame at Chicago's Art Institute
The Episcopal Church
The Brookings Institution
Interfaith Center on Corporate Responsibility
Committee for National Security
The Peace Child Foundation

Youth Project
National Lawyers' Guild
Massachusetts Fair Share
Illinois Public Action Council
Council on Economic Priorities
Economic Policy Institute

Roger Stryeski of Roselle, New Jersey, says, "I have a list for a War Crimes Tribunal when the Free Enterprise Revolution comes":

The Department of Religious Studies at the University of North Carolina, Chapel Hill: They may not be pinko but any organization as unknown as they are has to be dangerous.

Hogan Family, especially their knee-jerk comsymp shows on smoking and apartheid

New Jersey Hospital Association, for assisting the state in converting failing community hospitals to failing socialized ones

Charles Rose, newscaster

"Cousin Brucie" Morrow just because he is a %$#°–wipe

You're wrong about Charlie Rose, Roger. I bumped into him not long ago at a Popeye's Fried Chicken restaurant. No liberal eats Popeye's fried chicken for lunch without an immediate fatal coronary.

Anthony Esposito of Margate, Florida, keeps it brief and to the point:
Sally Jessy Raphael

Thomas Edwin Walker of La Porte, Texas, scolds:
Bono
"Bobcat" Goldthwait
R.E.M.
Molly Ivins

Who's another friend of mine, albeit a darned liberal one. I told you something like this would happen, Molly.

David A. Stephens of Pecos, Texas, is very mad at:
Frank Sesno
Charles Beerbarrel [sic]
Richard Simmons
Media Pains in the Ass in general
Any self-proclaimed scientist who lends his name to idiotic and flawed studies which advance his agenda: As someone with a bit of training

in science it offends me deeply to have "Dr." this and "Professor" that lending their names to something purely political—for example, that infantile nuclear winter model.

Any organization with the words "Peoples'" or "Concerned" in its name

Luddites

Douglas Hurd

François Mitterrand

Helmut Kohl

Leader of the German Greens Petra Kelly: If she wants to sit naked in the weeds and eat dandelions, let her.

People who use locutions like "entitlement," implying that others have a right to pick my pocket

People who use "Native American": What am I, a potted plant? I was born and reared in Texas.

People who debase English by destroying words such as "prejudice" and "quality"

Anyone whom W. S. Gilbert didn't like, excepting Sir Arthur Sullivan

People who produce commercials which scroll text on the screen and then read it to you

People who don't take free advice (in my case, on computers) but bang your ear anyway and then buy what the Radio Shack salesman says to

Friends, or rather onetime friends, who invite you to a party and then you discover they've become "were [as in werewolf] Amways"

People who chant, listen to, or produce any sort of rap whatsoever

People who ask you the same question three times, thinking that you will interim become Enlightened and know the answer

People who make commercials that show a dog eating and expect you to watch it with interest

People who expect you to develop your cat's palate

People who market scented and printed toilet paper

James A. Damask of Akron, Ohio, takes to task:

Anyone who uses the word "bonding" in reference to anything except epoxy glue

Anyone who uses the word "parenting"

Anyone who uses the word "wellness"

The entire cast of thirtysomething

Anyone who uses the word "ethnocentric"

Anyone who drives a car with a bumper sticker that reads, "You can't hug a child with nuclear arms"

Anything "New Age"

Rep. Tom Sawyer (D-OH)

Rep. Tony Hall (D-OH)

Anyone who wears or otherwise affiliates his person with a "peace" sign

Bookstores which carry Mother Jones, Pravda, *and* Soviet Life *but not the* American Spectator

Anyone whose eyes gleam when he says "bran"

The Philosophy Department at every state university

The American Friends Service Committee

The Central American Solidarity Association (CASA)

Anything "Quaker" which ain't oats

Anyone who uses the word "dialogue" when talking about foreign policy

Any female who uses the word "commitment": Okay, they ain't necessarily subversive, but I don't like them.

Anyone who uses the word "compassion" when talking about foreign policy

Anybody who compared the massacre of students in Peking to Kent State

VH-1

Anyone who uses the phrase "social justice"

Tom Ealey of Findlay, Ohio, cavils at:

United Methodist Bishops: any connection to the United Methodist Church is merely coincidental.

Rep. Mary Rose Oakar (D-OH)

and asks, "By the way, what is *'Tikkun'*?" [Beats my pair of jacks, Tom. Wlady Pleszczynski snuck it into the list.]

Dr. Dennis J. Doolin, who lives in Tokyo, deplores:

Warren Beatty

Sister Boom-Boom

The entirety of Castro Street in San Francisco

Everyone who orders "Perrier with a twist"

Every reviewer who disliked Tom Wolfe's The Bonfire of the Vanities

Michael G. Smith, address unknown, looks askance at:

Dr. Seuss

Most people who call themselves "Dr." but don't practice medicine

The Greenpeace mailing list
Ralph Moyed, pinkish columnist for the Wilmington newspaper
Denver, Colorado
99 percent of college daily newspaper editors
My ex-girlfriend, if her outlook hasn't changed by the time she's thirty

Timothy A. Curry of Seattle, Washington, objurgates:
Susan Brownmiller: for writing *Against Our Will,* the women's
    movement's *Mein Kampf*
Carl Sagan and Jonathan Schell, purveyors of nuclear winter, the most
    important scientific theory since phlogiston, phrenology, and the
    Piltdown Man
Tommy Smothers: Remember him telling brother Dick "Mom always
    liked you best"? Remember thinking Mrs. Smothers was no dummy?
Ted Turner, the only known human capable of producing a documentary
    on the Soviet Union so smarmy that the KGB was moved to apologize
    for it

Luke Asbury of Mill Valley, California, is steamed. He says, "You omitted":
Sen. Howard Metzenbaum (D-OH), the most vicious enemy the Bill of
    Rights has ever faced, with his criminally insane campaign to abolish
    Individual Freedom to defend one's Person, Family, Home, and
    Country, and restrict firearm ownership to the Police State and the thugs
"Also," says Luke,
The entire California legislature, mostly a pack of bumblewits and/or
    poltroons
"And, sadly," he continues,
President George Bush, who broke his word and sided with the "Don't
    Burn the Flag—Burn the Bill of Rights!" media dupes
This is George's second citation on the List (multiple mentions allowed because
he's a former Chief Executive). Maybe somebody in the White House should
have a look at the effect President Have-Half had on the We-Ain't-Taking-It
part of his constituency.

Thomas F. Steele of Orange County, California, has only one name for the
docket but, as Tom says, "It's an eye-opener for the most populous Republican
county in the country to contain such a critter":
Mayor of Irvine, California, Larry Agran, honors grad U.C. Berkeley,
    Harvard Law School, close friend of Tom Hayden, co-author of the
    California Bilateral Nuclear Weapons Freeze Initiative, executive

director of the Center for Innovative Diplomacy, which has set up
eighty Nicaragua/U.S. "sister city" relationships

"I didn't know Nicaragua *had* eighty cities," notes Tom. Neither did I, but Larry Agran is welcome to go be mayor of all of them.

L. C. Carter of El Paso, Texas, inveighs against:
Rose Kennedy, and the fruits of her womb

A group of self-described "militant right-wingers in Kentucky" submit a rather peculiar roster which combines politics, music criticism, and an apparent attempt to get even on some ill-advised sports betting:

The Rainbow Coalition
Mayor Ed Koch
Sen. James Exxon [sic] (D-NE)
Andy Rooney
Diane Sawyer
Paul Kirk
Michael Jackson, the singer, not the radio talk show host
John Hinckley, Jr.
Kitty Dukakis
Senate Majority Leader George Mitchell (D-ME)
The Grateful Dead
Joan Rivers
Metallica
Richard Daley
Union Boss Richard Trumka
Flag Burners
Abortionists [I must disagree here. I'm all for abortion, of the
    retroactive kind.]
AC/DC
Alice Cooper
Martina Navratilova
Don King
Lane Kirkland
Muhammad Ali
Toyotas [Toyotas?]
Ozzy Osbourne
KISS
Kareem Abdul-Jabbar
California Lt. Gov. Gray Davis
William "The Refrigerator" Perry

Jane Wyman: She divorced Reagan. How smart can she be? [Let us pause here to note that practically every member of the Reagan household except the Gipper himself has been named to the Enemies List. More quality time with the family, Ronald, please.]

Anthrax

Tone Loc

Draft dodgers [Hey, fellows, this cuts a bit close to the knuckle for some of us sixties-era born-again conservatives.]

Jeanne Dixon

"The sooner we can get out a contract on the following," says Thomas H. Black of Midland, Michigan, "the sooner we can all get to work on the plan to 'clean up the environment'":

John Catennacci

Day care

Sammy Davis, Jr.

Eckankar

Sonya Freedman

Squeaky Fromme

Bishop Gumbleton

Oveta Culp Hobby

IMF

Alfred Kinsey

John McEnroe

Bette Midler

Liza Minnelli

Muammar Qaddafi

Burt Reynolds

Rowan and Martin

The other Smothers Brother

J. D. Salinger

Bo Schembechler

Liv Ullman

Truman Capote

ERA

Dianne Feinstein

Sen. Daniel Inouye (D-HI)

Sen. Carl Levin (D-MI)

Joni Mitchell

Nicki McWhirter
Dean Martin
Manuel Noriega
G. Bromley Oxnam
Abu Nidal
Alan Quartermaine
Morley Safer
Tex Schramm
Jimmy Swaggart
Foster Wynans
Katharine Hepburn
David Brinkley
Patti Davis
Doris Day
Sally Field
The Federal Reserve System
The Gabor family
Amy Irving
Coretta King
Robin Leach
James Taylor
Daniel Ortega
Monica Quartermaine
Carl Rogers
Sylvester Stallone
Angela Sombranno
Tracey Ullman
X-rated movies
Vidal Sassoon

C. Collins of the American Enterprise Institute cries down:
Norbert Nadel
The Cincinnati Reds: a cheap shot, but one can't be too careful
Jose Canseco and any other major league player who charges for autographs: This is an obvious Commie plot to debase America's native game
Jim McMahon and Brian Bosworth: just because they're horrible people
Red Auerbach and John Thompson: ditto

Bruce Springsteen, another multimillionaire wailing about the
   wretchedness of capitalism
Harry Belafonte
Spike Lee
E. L. Doctorow
Bill Plante
Arthur Kropp
The post-containment George Kennan
Joseph Rauh
Andreas Papandreou
Hans-Dietrich Genscher
France
Neil Kinnock
David Lynch
Robert Hawke
*Any student who comes here because his backwater, tinhorn, Third
   World wasteland of a country can't provide a decent education and
   then complains about what a repressive and horrible system we
   have*
Robert Mapplethorpe
Would-be Armand Hammer Dwayne O. Andreas

John Paul Arnerich of Los Angeles, California, exprobates:
Mark Russell
Bill Press, California liberal sophist
David Gergen
The Detroit Pistons

Michael R. Hemmerich of Cleveland, Ohio, disparages:
Dick Cavett
Men who wear sandals
American Spectator *House Hoosiers:* OK, OK, just kidding!
Peter Hart
Nan Aron
Norman Ornstein
William Wimpisinger
People whose movements are engaged in a "struggle"

Indignant Methodist Thomas Donelson of Olathe, Kansas, writes "to
nominate":

The Reverend George Baldwin
"to your New Enemies List. Mr. Baldwin spoke in front of the Kansas East Conference of the United Methodist Church about Nicaragua and the workers' paradise being developed there.

"Five years ago, Mr. Baldwin took a vow of poverty and moved to Managua where a vow of poverty has been easy to undertake ever since the Sandinistas took over running the economy. Despite his vow of poverty, he is going on a world's tour for peace with someone else footing the bill."

Leo Eagle of Old Bethpage, New York, tells us, "Long Island has its own brand of lefties. I say off with their heads":
  Rep. Thomas Downey (D-Amityville)
  Rep. Robert Mrazek (D-Centerport)
  Rep. George Hochbrueckner (D-Coram)

"Red" Michaels of Birmingham, Alabama, is furious with any number of people, including some local Alabamians I've never heard of. But have at 'em, Red. We're here to serve:
  Roy Higginbotham
  Arthur D. Penser (Huntsville)
  Frank Sievelmann (Fayette)
  Earl Hilliard
  Crumm Foshee
  Richard Arrington
  Alvin Holmes
  Thomas Reed
  Ted Bryant
  Abraham Woods
  Mary Jean Haddin
  Mitch Mendelson
  Frank Bruer
  John Brinkley
  Rheta Grimsley Johnson
And this cryptic addition:
  Sieglemann
Also:
  Henry Kissinger
  Jaruzelski
  Sen. Richard Shelby (D-AL)
  Sen. Howell Heflin (D-AL)

Art Buchwald
Robert T. Stafford
Sen. John Chafee (D-RI)
Sen. Dale Bumpers (D-AR)
Rep. J. Oberstar (D-MN)
Sen. Al D'Amato (R-NY)
Sen. Mark Hatfield (R-OR)
Sen. Bob Packwood (R-OR)

Bruce Poindexter of Ann Arbor, Michigan, berates:
The editorial staff of the Michigan Daily
The entire state of Minnesota
The California condor
The snail darter
The two whales freed from the ice in Alaska

Larry J. King of Morrisville, Vermont, has an unusual venue of criticism. "I don't believe you'll recognize any of the following names," he says:
Alan Moore: His works include an attack on the Reagan administration nuclear policy. He belongs to the British organization AARGH (Artists Against Rampant Government Homophobia).
Frank Miller is afraid that the religious right intends to censor his work.
Danny O'Neil criticized mankind's treatment of the environment in a recent editorial and has written a story condemning the conservative churches' involvement in politics.
George Perez wrote a story in which a woman tells her "gay" brother to be proud of what he is. Mr. Perez is a committed feminist.
"What do these people have in common?" Larry asks, rhetorically. "They write comic books. Here's some more data for you to chew on:
"1. Gloria Steinem is the consultant on the 'Wonder Woman' comic written by George Perez.
"2. In Superman comics, one of Superman's best friends, Maggie Sawyer, is a lesbian.
"3. One comic used to be called 'Justice League of America' until the 'America' part of the title was removed in the interests of one-worldism."

Greg Paolano of Centereach, New York, chides:
Anyone who runs against Jesse Helms

Kip Krady, director of Accuracy in Media's speakers bureau, reprehends:
Cartoonist Feiffer, Jules
Neo-Nazi thugs everywhere and their skinhead brethren

Paul Seabury of Berkeley, California, declaims upon:
Alger Hiss
*Right Reverend Barbara Harris, Suffaragan Bishop of the Diocese of
Massachusetts*: The Rt. Rev. is a lesbian, a nuclear unilateralist, a
Sandalista, a kind of theological Ron Dellums. She was never entrusted
with a parish before becoming bishop, probably because no parish would
take her.

Jan Beck of Seattle, Washington, dresses down:
Stanley Kramer
Defense Attaché
Legal Services Corp.
Gary Merrill
Parade *magazine* [You're wrong, Jan. And ex–Marine Viet Vet Walter
Anderson, who runs *Parade,* will probably be glad to tell you so in
person.]
Riverside Community Church
Seattle City Council, for voting Managua a "sister city," inviting the
Soviets to "Friendship Games," etc.
60 Minutes
*Anyone using the terms "red-baiting," "Commie-bashing" or
"McCarthyism" without quotation marks*

Finally, *American Spectator* staff assistant Dan Erech weighs in with:
"President" Carlos Duque of Panama
Mayor W. Wilson Goode of Philadelphia
Edward Dos Santos, MPLA leader, Angola
Rep. Barney Frank's "significant other"
Anyone dumb enough to vacation in Lebanon [Hey, watch it, kid.]
Craig Spence and "Professional Services"
Li Peng
Prime Minister Michael Manley of Jamaica
Javier Perez de Cuellar
Walter

I would also like to thank Joseph P. Maguire of Evanston, Illinois; Mercedes
Casey of Lake Charles, Louisiana; Louis J. Tripoli of Rochester, New York;
Joe Mysak of New York, New York; and Mrs. M. B. Hermel, all of whose
choices for incrimination had already been incriminated by others.

And there was one final letter which contained a photocopy of the *American Spectator* subscription ad that lists many of the fine, thoughtful people who read our publication. My own name was added to the top of that list and, at the bottom, in crude, shaky letters appeared the message "KILL THEM ALL." OK, Mom, cut it out. ❖

IV

Shoot
the
Wounded

The American Spectator, November 1990

Springs

Well, fellow witch-hunters, a lot has happened since we began our New Enemies List. Freedom has come to Eastern Europe, the Soviet Union has shriveled as a world power, the people of Nicaragua have given Danny Ortega the Order of the Boot, and all because of us and our brave revival of the Red Scare. As a result of our noble crusade, Communists are now just another small, half-baked cult who put out an occasional newsletter (the *Washington Post,* for instance) and pester people in airports (particularly Peking's). Tail-Gunner Joe must have a mile-wide smile up there in Heaven's AA meeting.

"But who ya gonna pick on now?" smirk the liberals, who are no smarter running with the hares in the nineties than they were hunting with the hounds in the seventies. The answer to their question of who we're going to pick on now is—them. Let's whoop on the useful idiots, the moral equivalentizers, the peace scum, the social justice hairballs, and see who sang the Marxist tune and expected us not to mind because they had the lyrics wrong. You're next, you south-ends-of-an-NEA-grant-headed-north, you.

We won't be able to print all the additions to the Scroll of Fools this year, partly because of sheer volume, partly because we've already shot so many of the fish in the barrel, and partly because we've exhausted the earth's supply of "Fonda Commies" puns. Although we hounded Mitch Snyder to his death—he's got a home now, and a warm one at that—we have yet to settle on fit punishment for our blacklist victims. Reader suggestions range from the bloodthirsty ("Throw them into a pit of live lawyers") to the excessively humane ("Put them out of their misery with a brick"). No doubt a happy medium will emerge.

First off, we will exercise *droit du seigneur* and set a couple of burning faggots (no sniggering, please) at the feet of Satan's familiars:
- *The twig-toothing leaf-brains who spray-painted my local McDonald's with the message "Meat Is Murder"*— If meat is murder, does that mean eggs are rape?
- *The freshly unemployed Neville Chamberlains at Nuclear Free America,* who proposed replacing the Iron Curtain with a "Curtain of Peace and Freedom." I guess if you're caught trying to escape through the "Peace Curtain" you get petitioned to death. Among the various frisbee-witted individuals and organizations "who wholeheartedly endorse this proposal" are:
  International Philosophers for Prevention of Nuclear Omnicide: I am not kidding.
  Nevada Desert Experience: I am still not kidding.
  Center on War and the Child
  International Peace Academy

Lawyers Alliance for Nuclear Arms Control: Quick, which is worse, lawyers or nuclear winter?

Albert Einstein International Academy Foundations: After the guy who gave us the mushroom cloud

Hungarian Reform Federation: No wonder it took them so long to reform Hungary . . . they were in the wrong country.

Coretta Scott King

Professionals for National Security: Which begs the question, "How do I go about joining Amateurs for International Insecurity?"

So much for the goofs, now let's turn to the goons:

Third World Caucus/Clergy and Laity Concerned

This bunch sent me a press release, trying to convince me to publish the name of the "Central Park Jogger." What I'll gladly publish is the coffin measurements for the filthy little jackals who almost killed her. But let me quote, with one obvious omission, from the TWC/CALC press release:

> Our national group has voted to make known its concerns regarding the increase [sic] racist collaboration between the newspapers and the so-called justice system. . . .
>
> Concerted efforts on the part of newspapers to treat people of color in an insensitive and completely different manner than which European suspects and victims are written about is criminal. . . .
>
> There are a number of cases we can refer to, but the current cases of Tawana Brawley and XXX, known to the world as the Central Park Jogger, are two cases in point. Both were found near death after being assaulted. Tawana, 16, should not have had her body exposed to the world in public. There was & is a concerted effort not to publish the name of the older European, XXX. . . .

Third World Caucus/Clergy and Laity Concerned's address is 198 Broadway, New York, New York 10038, and I am sure they would appreciate suggestions on where to place their future press releases.

Next on my personal Enemies List are

Conservative Democrats

because they're always getting caught in bed with Ted Kennedy and telling us, "It's OK—we're not in love." Besides, everybody hates liberal Democrats these days. Of course, being good liberals, they hate themselves, too.

Last, but most of all, *j'accuse*:

> *Everyone mentioned in the book* Tenured Radicals: How Politics Has
> Corrupted Our Higher Education, *by Roger Kimball, except*
> *Roger Kimball*

When it comes to throwing the book at the stinking, treasonous redniks in our universities, this is the book to throw. Mortarboards off to you, Rog.

Before I go, kudos to Polish painter Franciszek Starowieyski, who founded his own McCarthy Society in Warsaw and told the Polish weekly *Przekroj:*

> The McCarthy Society is my private society, created to honor this fine man who halted the frenzied advance of Communism turning brains into jelly. That is what his greatness is based on. This is a very elite society. I don't even remember if anyone else besides me belongs to it.

And now, the New Enemies List Update:

L et us begin on a spiritual note, with five additions from Noel K. Anderson, pastor at the First Presbyterian Church in Edmond, Oklahoma. The reading shall be from the Book of Deuteronomy 32:15:

> But Jeshurun waxed fat, and kicked: thou art waxen fat, thou art grown thick, thou art covered with fatness; then he forsook God which made him, and lightly esteemed the Rock of his salvation.

The Reverend Anderson would now like us to bow our heads and say a small prayer for these people and institutions as they walk that long, lonely mile to the ducking stool:

> *Self-righteous nonsmokers*
> *All seminaries which mean to conventionalize "inclusive language,"*
> *sodomists' rights, and a "Theology of Compensation" for any*
> *self-proclaiming oppressed group*
> *John Irving,* for his vacuous and inapposite political whimperings in
> *A Prayer for Owen Meany*
> *Any office with more plants than people*
> *Sensitive people who dress like gypsies or peasants*

Helen H. Bergman of New York, New York, indicts the Big Apple's entire Democratic party establishment and lists most of them. Here are some highlights from her *nomenklatura* of worms in the winesap:

All the West Side Reform Democratic Clubs of Manhattan
Local 1199, Hospital Workers Union
Barry Feinstein of the Teamsters Union
Sandra Feldman of the United Federation of Teachers
Stanley Hia of AFSCME
Jay Mazur of the ILGWU
Elizabeth Holtzman
Ruth Messinger

Howard W. Whetzel of Pittsburgh, Pennsylvania, warns us that our current strategy against Boob Nation is misguided. "All rabble multiply exponentially," he says. "Elimination by individual identity will necessarily result in defeat. . . . I propose going to the heart of the matter: the breeders. To wit":

Women with two last names
Male teachers of American History under fifty-eight years of age
All teachers of "Health"
All school boards whose school hours are determined by a bus drivers'
    contract

Tim Ferguson of the *Wall Street Journal* sends a memo saying simply:
Presidential spouses and offspring
Which seems a bit rough on Barbara and Millie.

An anonymous source at UCLA nominates:
Physicians for Social Responsibility: May they all get a large dose of
    socialized medicine right where they deserve it.

Roy Marokus, who's an M.D. but no Bolshie croaker, writes in to protest the inclusion, in a previous Enemies List, of his hometown of Dayton, Ohio. "Wait," says Dr. Marokus. "Now that I think about it . . .":
Phil Donahue used to do morning egg market quotations on Channel 7
    . . . and that drip
Martin Sheen went to Chaminade High School.
Sorry, Doc.

Terry Przybylski of Des Plaines, Illinois, would like to put the Enemies List on the Enemies List. "How," he asks, "could you do this to me? After I went to all the trouble of submitting such a splendid enemies list, you quoted me as naming 'Marvin Miller, the former head of the *basketball* players union'!!!!" Mr. Przybylski points out that the "cloddish Miller" is the former head of the *baseball* players union and blames this error, quite rightly, on an excess of Hoosier hoop-heads on the *American Spectator* staff.

Mark Saucier of Gulfport, Mississippi, who claims that he likes Frank Zappa and dislikes George Bush too much to ever be a conservative, writes to us anyway, to condemn:

> *Andrea Dworkin,* whose all-sex-is-rape theorem transcends all common sense in an effort to make the male of the species look like the cretinous, barbaric ape-devils that we truly are, aren't we?

Stay as sweet as you are, Mark.

M ike Northrup, whose handwriting renders his hometown in Maryland illegible, names:

> *The Maryland State Employees United Charity Campaign,* for allowing the *Maryland Nuclear Weapons Freeze Education Fund* to be listed in its contributors' guide as a charity

An anonymous correspondent from "The People's Republic of Oregon" proposes:

> *Any journalist, commentator, or other fool who refers to the old guard in Moscow or Peking as "conservatives"*
> *Whoever invented the brassiere and put the hooks in the back*
> *Every state with state-run liquor stores*

Ms. or Mr. X continues: "After six days and a few twelve-packs spent in deep reflection, I believe I have a non-cruel, unusual punishment for the condemned. *. . . Give them what they want!"*

We're cold-hearted conservatives here at the *American Spectator.* Heck, we have to call a Frigidaire service representative to get an EKG. But giving liberal bed wetters what they claim to desire is too callous even for us. Imagine Pamela Harriman trapped in a world where everyone had to do her own laundry. We shudder.

Don Lynch of Arlington, Virginia, condemns:

> *Demagogic Southern senators and congressmen who are mislabeled "conservative"*
> *Conservatives who call discrimination "affirmative action" and pro-death people "pro-choice"*
> *People who call things like alcoholism, drug abuse, and poverty a "disease"*

Sorry we didn't print your letter sooner, Don, but we were "sick."

Charles Perry of Sylmar, California, singles out:
  Gloria Allred, the Church Lady of the Left, fuming defender of gay foster parents and triumphant integrator of boring men's clubs

J. Edgar Williams of Carrboro, North Carolina, sends no candidates of his own but has some valuable suggestions about where to go to look for *auto-da-fé* fodder: "There are several sources I find valuable. . . . The Isaacs' *Coercive Utopians;* Brownfeld and Walker's *The Revolution Lobby;* Powell's *Covert Cadre;* Collier and Horowitz's *Destructive Generation;* and Tyson's *Prophets for Useful Idiots.*" Mr. Williams also mentions a *Biographical Dictionary of the Left* but notes that the work was published in 1969 and is somewhat out of date.
  A few of us neo-types at the *American Spectator* sincerely hope we aren't in there.

Tom Gordon, address unknown, hands a page of the Bible with a large black spot in the middle to:
  John Cougar Mellencamp: his fulminations on the family farm, racism, the working man, unions, and Vietnam vets—did Mr. Mellencamp serve?—are wearing very thin
  Lou Reed, who finds the time to pose for American Express ads when he's not bemoaning American greed and selfishness

"Enjoyed reading your enemies list . . . until I noticed that you use those awful two-capital-letter state abbreviations that the post office thought up so addresses can be read by robots," writes Dale E. Elliott, who lives in IL.

Richard A. Showstead of Boston, Massachusetts, moots:
  Sigmund Freud, cokehead
  Anna Freud, daddy dearest
  B. F. Skinner, redneck

Philip Averbuck of Watertown, Massachusetts, drops a dime on:
  Randolph Ryan, a writer for the commie *Boston Globe*
Mr. Averbuck encloses a column by Comrade Ryan in which the FMLN terrorists in El Salvador are quoted using surfer slang. Hang ten, maybe. Hang Randolph, definitely.

Eddie Page of Crawfordville, Florida, thinks P. J. O'Rourke should go to the head of the Enemies List for his admitted friendship with arbitrarily nonlisted liberals Pat Schroeder and Michael Kinsley. P.J. says, Watch your back,
  Eddie Page

Another wannabe self-nominee is Molly Gill of St. Petersburg, Florida, who signs herself "Editor, *Independent Woman,*" beneath which, in parentheses, she puts "Feminist Newsletter," as though, with that title, we might suppose *Independent Woman* to be a trade journal of the offshore oil-drilling industry or something. "'The New Enemies List' is very funny," says Ms. Gill. "I can only conclude that the majority of your readers suffer from irregularity. P.S. You now have somebody else to hate." Not at all, Ms. Gill. We consider you a valuable source of intellectual roughage.

K urt D. Baumgardner of Smyrna, Georgia, is not at all amused by recrudescent McCarthyism. He cancels his subscription to the *American Spectator* and says, "I can think of few things that disgust me more than the thought of a return to the time when the prejudiced opinions of a few immoral power-seekers gripped the nation with fear." Yes, Mr. Baumgardner, we're upset by the Mayor Barry verdict, too, but shouldn't you be taking this up with the *Nation?*

Bob Foster of Purcellville, Virginia, would put paid to:
   Anybody whose car sports one or more of the following bumper stickers:
      Think Globally / Act Locally
      Test Peace / Not Nuclear Weapons
      If You Want Peace / Work for Justice
      Love Animals / Don't Eat Them
   Demonstrators who go limp when arrested

"May someone from the Caribbean backwoods propose some members for the 'Hall of Shame'?" asks Carlos F. Mendoza-Tio of Santurce, Puerto Rico. His choices:
   The (dis)Honorable Ron De Lugo (D-Virgin Islands)
   The (dis)Honorable Jaime Fuster (D-Puerto Rico)
"These two scoundrels," says Mendoza-Tio, "are in cahoots to torpedo the proposed plebiscite for Puerto Rico, effectively disenfranchising millions of American citizens."

Jonathan J. Cohen of Brookline, Massachusetts, writes on behalf of the *American Spectator's* Zionist wing, saying, quite reasonably, "We Jewish righties have to be careful when making such a list. Certain bona fide lefties can be absolved if they're hard-line supporters of Israel. Thus, we spared Alan Dershowitz, Representatives Tom Lantos and Steve Solarz, Charles Krauthammer (and most of the *New Republic* gang), and—yes—Barney Frank. Although the last may be back on other grounds." Mr. Cohen amends:

Pat Buchanan: because of his infamous anti-Semitic remarks inspired by the Auschwitz convent flap. I *tried* to like Paddy-boy, but he's a regular Father Coughlin.
Ah, Jonathan me lad, imagine a whole family of them the way yours truly has got.

And, speaking of the Harps, John F. Curran of River Edge, New Jersey, would list:
Everyone responsible in any way for the Calvin Klein Obsession commercials on TV
"We should talk to the Japanese," says himself. "Our televisions should be designed to recognize these incoming signals and to *explode,* rather than permit these assaults on the human soul to enter our homes."

Bryan R. Johnson of Blacksburg, Virginia, complains about the response to his previous contributions to the Enemies List:

Imagine my pride and extreme nervousness when I found my name and current location published in the *American Spectator.* I mean, I'll stand behind my list against all comers (particularly since I'm more heavily armed than any of the people on my list) but the *American Library Association* has some pretty tough characters. . . . I loaded Mr. Shotgun with #4 buck (more effective than 00—more pellets per load and a better pattern) and kept it within reach at all times. Then, I waited. And waited. Nothing. Nada. Zilch. . . . Is it possible that the left actually got the joke?"

No.

Ed Rice, who's keeping his address to himself, sends us a note of clarification:

In the November 1989 installment of your Enemies List you include the *Greenpeace mailing list.* I'm on it but I'm innocent! Back in the spring my twelve-year-old Brittany spaniel, Jack, treed a Greenpeace canvasser. To avoid the trouble, I gave the guy a couple of bucks. . . . P.S. Can we put Jack in for an award or medal or something?

Paul Hagstrom of San Francisco, California, would gladly sic Jack on:
Mr. Herb Caen, San Francisco columnist for whom clans, cults, and perverts come under the category of sacred special-interest groups. All except God-fearing, church-going Christians.
Any and all who go around "feeling good about themselves"

Carol Ann Calamia of Rochester, New York, does not feel anything like that way about:
The New York Times Magazine
"An enemies list could be constructed with all the people featured in the magazine alone," says Ms. Calamia.

Kenneth M. Mason, also of Rochester, would like to turn in to the authorities:
Gregory Peck, that great American who did so much to assassinate
Robert Bork's character, narrating the "commercial" that so many TV stations saw fit to play as a news item

Thomas D. Watt of Omaha, Nebraska, drops a line just to let us know that "a fitting punishment for the loony left is to make them commit to memory the newspaper columns of Mary McGrory." Please, please, Mr. Watt, there's such a thing as the Eighth Amendment.

Daniel Rodriguez, who sojourns in this mortal vale of woe (that is, Washington, D.C.) but who is careful to point out he's "formerly of Texas," looks askance at:
Nuclear-free Takoma Park, Maryland
White singers with fake Jamaican accents
City slickers who speak like country folk (like Ann Richards and Molly Ivins)

Daniel Young of Ottawa, Canada, would make a burnt offering of:
HUD
The California Raisins
Teenage homosexual encounter groups
Tupperware parties
Publicly funded health care
Canadian artists who move to the U.S. to make dollars and return to Canada once a year to share their anti-American views

Mark Katzenbaum of Arlington, Virginia, takes a swing at:
Anyone who uses only one name
He points out that rock stars who use one name were on a previous Enemies List but says, "We can't forget Cher and Lucifer."

Donna Marmorstein of Aberdeen, South Dakota, unloads on:
Whoever invented illiteracy billboards
The left half of Joan Beck

Burger King's marketing company: the one that came up with the
"Sometimes ya just gotta break the rules" ad
Educated people who use "impact" as a verb
Makers of sugar-saturated, additive-laced children's cereals
Makers of whole-grained, oat-branned, vitamin-encrusted adult cereals
Any church whose name begins with "United"
Anyone who believes in deconstructionism, semiotics, and critical thinking
without being able to define each term in fewer than fifty words
Drug education programs that equate coffee, aspirin, and cough drops
with pot, heroin, and crack
Whoever named last October "Head Injury Awareness Month"

Kent Gordis of Geneva, Switzerland, sends a rueful missive saying, "There
is no corner of the earth so remote or bucolic that it does not contain candidates
for the New Enemies List." And he sends us two from Switzerland:
Jean Zeigler, a socialist member of the Swiss parliament who accused
Nestlé of having conspired with the CIA in the overthrow of Salvador
Allende
Franz Weber, who devised and animated the gigantic campaign to "save the
baby seals," enlisting Brigitte Bardot and other celebrities, thereby
amassing his fortune

While we've got the animals in our crosshairs, let's listen up to David A.
Stephens of Pecos, Texas, who says:
Peckerheads here who claim one shouldn't shoot coyotes!

Alan N. Cowan of Australia turns the dingos loose upon:
Senior executives of U.N. agencies (usually Scandinavians) who jet
around the world in first-class luxury and sanctimoniously lecture the
Western democracies on the need to do more for the poor

Professors Pam Brown and Gary Anderson, from the Economics Department
at California State University in Northridge, plant the sharp ends of their analyt-
ical skills in the hides of:
People concerned with empowerment
All Nobel Peace Prize laureates
Most economics Nobel prizewinners
Anyone who knows what tofu is

Wendy Connors, address unknown, suggests:
People who cheat the welfare system
The welfare system

Anthony Hasek, of the Toronto office of the commendable Canadian organization Conservative Insight, sends us a list of frozen northerners who should be further chilled:

The entire Progressive Conservative Party, an oxymoron full of morons.
Canada's $100 million loan to China after *Tiananmen*
Anyone Canadians call a "national treasure," usually because they're
    hauling down the big bucks in the States and are lauded by American
    pinkos
Quebec separatists
Philippe Ruston, a lunatic head-measurer who claims that Orientals are
    genetically superior to whites, and that whites are in turn superior to
    blacks
Americans who fled up here with their tails between their legs in the
    1960s
Americans who fled up here with their tails between their legs in the
    1980s
Americans I've met while traveling who:
    wear Canadian flags on their luggage so they can hitchhike and not
        get blown up
    say what a great country we have, having never been here
    don't know Canada is not another state

"P.S.," says Mr. Hasek. "Don't just open your floodgates to the Great White North either. Send all your lefties to Alabama—they'll know what to do with them."

Here is a heartrending letter from one James R. Erwin who, understandably, does not give his address:

I love my wife, don't get me wrong. But it's a mixed marriage (she has liberal tendencies; myself I'm still a YAF member in good standing). On the eve of our ninth anniversary, I feel compelled to denounce her, in the hope it may shock her into reality. I've tried reading the *Spectator* to her . . . but with a mocking laugh she says things like "Reagan on the rock . . . HA!" For the list:
    Sharon D. Erwin
I pray I'm not too late to help her; naturally, I will go wherever the Committee finds it necessary to send her, and will continue to read the

Spectator to her until her soul is revived. Please give this request top priority; the political future of my six-year-old daughter weighs heavily on my mind.

Rest easy, Mr. Erwin. Just leave everything to Dr. Bob Tyrrell and Nurse P.J.

Scott Rains of Indianapolis, Indiana, wishes to include:
> *Terre Haute Mayor Pete Chalos,* for being the dumbest liberal in the
> world

We'd all been wondering who that was.

Lawrence M. Heavey, Jr., doesn't say where he's from, but we surmise it's one of the nicer suburbs. He condemns:
> *Businessmen who wear jogging shoes with their suits on their way to and
> from the train station*

A mysterious stranger called "Vulca" delivered this message: "I use here the name Vulca. Vulca was the Etruscan architect who built the first public buildings in Rome, thus providing at least the material foundations of a great and noble civilization. But perhaps I should not say this, lest someone call me Eurocentric. Ha."
Vulca has it in for:
> *California quacks who say that good foods which have benefited us for
> several millennia, things like meat and milk, are harmful and full of
> "toxins" even as they promote their vegetarian diet and vitamin cults*
> *Anyone who calls swamp grass a health food*

Vulca has spoken.

Speaking of unusual communications, there is this from W. J. Provance of Murrieta, California: "I prevailed upon the Governing Board of the Secret Team . . . to allow me to provide you with a copy of their Standing Operating Plan No. 112228, 'The List.' I would like to tell you more about the Secret Team but everything is a secret. And we'd like to tell your readers about Plan No. 112228, but it's secret, too."

Charlotte Smith, from P.J.'s hometown of Toledo (How are the Mud Hens doing?), Ohio, says, "There's something wonderful about sweeping indictments," and sweepingly indicts:
> *People who say "awhnt" instead of "aunt" who weren't born in England*
> *Anybody fool enough to have been, or wish to have been, at Woodstock*
> *Liberals who breathlessly follow the doings of the Royal Family*

Jay Hass of Philadelphia, Pennsylvania, submits:

Primert
Avantor
Synovus
Crestar
Imtrex
Cenit
Centura
Sovran

"Incredibly," says Mr. Hass, "these are not chemical compounds, computer passwords, government agencies, or figures of classical mythology, but names with which fitted-shirt and tapered-slack members of boards have rechristened eight American *banks*. Whatever happened to names which told you something about the business or its clientele, such as Citizens and Southern, the Detroit Bank and Trust Company, and First and Merchants National Bank?"

"Why seine for minnows?" asks George M. Hollenback of Houston, Texas, an unrepentant Pelagian who believes in free will and personal responsibility.

> Go for a really big fish like *Augustine of Hippo* who screwed up Western civilization by laying the foundation for all leftist "isms" that plague it today. Big Brother and the Welfare State are both the inevitable result of his incessant whining about the innate rottenness and helplessness of man. Ditto for 'liberation theology' and pinko clerics who currently infest the Body of Christ.

Back with the minnow net is John C. McPherson of Mt. Ida, Arizona, lowering the boom on:

Anyone who compares the United States to "other industrial nations" for any purpose whatsoever
Police Chief Joseph McNamara of San Jose
The Police Foundation
Any cop who uses his title and uniform to front for liberal causes
Anyone attending a "silent vigil" at an execution
Anyone using the term "the new homeless" with a straight face
Anyone suggesting that we just don't pay enough taxes in this country

V. Maida of New York, New York, sends us the names of "a few more who need to be rooted out":

Animal rights activists who think hassling women on the street constitutes
a tremendous contribution to the planet: Why don't they pick a
fight with a Hell's Angel in a leather jacket?
Judge Stewart Hancock of the New York Court of Appeals, who reversed
the harassment conviction of some woman in upstate New York who
called a retarded woman a "bitch" and her son a "dog"
Elie Wiesel's hairstylist

A lady with the delightful—Howard W. Whetzel's opinion to the contrary—
name Angeli DiLucca-Paterson from Pasadena, California, scolds:
The inventor of the leaf blower
Any pro football player who gyrates, dances, high-steps, grabs another
player's rear end, or otherwise acts like an imbecile after a touchdown or
play

Lawrence P. Biacchi of Lancaster, Pennsylvania, provides us with the "Philo-
sopher's Enemies List":
Allan Bloom, for claiming Nietzsche runs the world
Francis Fukuyama, for digging up Hegel
Any guy who, at this moment, is planning to dig up Kant
Thank you, Mr. Biacchi, and allow us to refer you to the "International Philo-
sophers for Prevention of Nuclear Omnicide" cited in our introduction.

Daniel Buksa of Munster, Indiana, a Second Amendment fancier, berates:
Sarah Brady: Yeah, I'm sorry her husband got shot and is now a cripple,
but she doesn't have to take it out on the rest of us. And besides, if
anybody should have a gripe, it should be the Gipper. But he's still an
NRA supporter.
All of the rest of the confused legislators and supposed do-gooders who
have forgotten that the Second Amendment to the Constitution was
designed to prevent an oppressive government abusing the rights of
the people—so said Alexander Hamilton in *Federalist 29.* And so say
all of us.

Kyle Jorgenson from Kansas City, Missouri, gives the evil eye to:
U.S. District Judge Russell Clark: When the folks of K.C. voted against
raising property taxes, His Officiousness ordered us to increase our
property taxes by 91 percent to fund school busing.

A. G. Layton and "friends of the same ilk" from Canada aim their scorn both
high and low:

Erasmus of Rotterdam: sanctimonious hypocrite, the spiritual father of all
   cardiac hemophiliacs
Program Traders on the New York Stock Exchange: sworn enemies of the
   capitalist system, borers from within

Jim Dornan of Orange County, California, takes special exception to:
   Ron Kovic: Kovic . . . is considering a run for Congress against one of the
      foremost defenders of freedom in the House of Representatives, Bob
      Dornan . . .
Uh, Jim, not that we give a damn about conflicts of interest, but you wouldn't
happen to be any relation?

Leslie Woolf Hedley, editor and publisher of the Exile Press in Sonoma,
California, contributes "the following list of those . . . whose mental spasms
infected American culture":
   John Cage, because he is a brimborion
   Creative writing teachers
   Stanford University, because they hired and retain an idiot professor who
      loudly professes that the Holocaust was a Zionist-Hollywood lie
   Ezra Pound, because his insanity is still contagious
Mr. Hedley, if you think you're going to get us to admit we don't know what
"brimborion" means, you are sadly mistaken.

S teve Bodio, an old acquaintance from New Hampshire, has moved to
  Magdalena, New Mexico, and reports that that otherwise lovely state is
afflicted with:
   Santa Fe and all its residents and its "style"
   *People who moved to Bernalillo County and immediately banned the
      cockfighting that their neighbors had indulged in since 1500*
   Everybody who says "Native American": every non–bureaucratically
      employed Indian I know says "Indian."
   *Those who drive by grazed-out Indian lands and bitch about private
      cattlemen and their subsidies*
   Nouveau fly fishermen who scorn catfish
   Fishermen who claim fishing is not hunting
   The Albuquerque Journal, *a supposedly Republican daily with a* New
      York Times *editorial policy*
   Fake pickup trucks for yuppies

"Please," writes Billy Long of St. Petersburg, Florida, "delouse":
   The 94 senators who voted in favor of the "Hate Crimes" Bill S419

C. T. Hellmuth, president of C. T. Hellmuth & Associates Insurance Brokers of Chevy Chase, Maryland, takes a moment from his business day to rebuke the policies of:

Adlai Stevenson, who convinced JFK to deny promised air cover at the Bay of Pigs

The National Education Association's bureaucrats, the pernicious destroyers of American students' ability to compete in the world economy by their emphasis on "feel-good" subjects, de-emphasis of mathematics, English, and American history, and their denigration of competitive scholarship

Phil Donahue (Molly Yard in drag): He mouths the pacifist and militant feminist drivel that Marlo Thomas has spoon-fed him. Although he likes to pose as the high priest of militant feminism, in his heart he must realize that his brand of loony-left nihilism, America-bashing, and *True Confessions* exploitation of unfortunately disturbed human beings is a real putdown of intelligent feminists. He would not have a prayer of survival in any time slot where thoughtful viewers had other alternatives.

Arthur Schlesinger, who convinced JFK to stand idly by while the Berlin Wall was being built and then had the audacity to appear on the *Today Show* to discuss the wall's fall

Special Prosecutor Lawrence Walsh

And each of the attorneys who is now working, or has ever worked, with Walsh

And his or her law firms

Ralph Neas, the scabrous architect of the senatorial lynching of Judge Bork

Huyler E. Romond, Jr., of Mantoloking, New Jersey, says, with great indignation, "I live in Ocean County, one of the most Republican counties in New Jersey. Registered Republicans outnumber Democrats 63,339 to 47,059. However, due to gerrymandering, all my elected representatives above the county level are Democrats." Mr. Romond then lists them. We will see to it, sir. Their time grows short.

Ellen Blacksmith of Pittsburgh, Pennsylvania, fulminates against:

That demonic voice who did the Dukakis TV ads [She notes he's not properly out of work, as the Duke is: "He's been doing AT&T and other commercials."]

That little misfit who played McCorney in Roe v. Wade *on TV*

William Norman Grigg of Provo, Utah, has found scum on an unlikely pond—two professors at Brigham Young University:
> *Eugene England,* who, apparently in response to the opening of a
>   McDonald's in Moscow, lamented the fact that the Soviets have
>   "succumbed to American materialism and preference for speed over taste"
> *Ted Lyon,* who urges students to learn about the "positive aspects" of
>   Marxism, especially liberation theology, which he describes as linking
>   Marx and Christ in a "very holy union"

Gary Osen and Tom Propson, co-chairmen of the Robert Bork Legal Defense Fund at the George Washington University Law School, bring their guns to deck level and load with grape to fire on:
> *Louis Farrakhan,* for making us want to tolerate bigots just a bit
> *Hodding Carter,* for thinking he's smarter than George Will
> *Al Sharpton,* for forcing us to defend Mario Cuomo
> *The AFL-CIO,* for trying to tear off a hunk of Lech Walesa for themselves
> *Animal rights activists,* for irritating an already unstable and well-armed
>   segment of the population

An anonymous contributor sends us a flyer advertising the "Archbishop Romero March to End the U.S. War in Central America." Among the organizations listed as sponsoring this traipse of twits:
> *American Indian Movement*
> *DC SCAR (Student Coalition Against Racism)* [Winner of the Infelicitous
>   Acronym Award.]
> *United Church of Christ* [Again, Donna Marmorstein warned us about
>   churches whose names begin with "United."]
> *Young Koreans United* [Wrong continent, you guys.]
> *Penn Central America Solidarity Alliance* [We pledge to ride the train.]

Plus these oddly yclept Marching and Chowder Societies:
> *Consider the Alternatives*
> *Going Home*

And P.J.'s personal favorite:
> *Interfaith Office of Accompaniment*

Chris Phelps of Glendale, California, sends us a letter beginning, "I know what you're thinking. A little hasty, too broad a stroke, maybe it should be pared down. P.J., this *IS* the pared-down version." He encloses the entire campus telephone directory for the University of California at Berkeley.

Actually, Mr. Phelps, you are being quite unfair. In the faculty and staff section, in the midst of the *P*s, is one "Perkins, Karen K."—a postdoctoral fellow in microbiology who is the former girlfriend of P. J. O'Rourke, a brilliant woman (the "former" proves it), and a staunch conservative.

Camilo O'Kuinghttons, Jr., of San Francisco, California, provides us with our first evidence of Enemies List plagiarism. The Kenneth Cole clothing store ran an ad in the *San Francisco Examiner* headlined, "Some of the people not invited to the opening of our new store," followed by a list. Bad enough that Kenneth Cole should crib from us, but his list turned out to contain many of our most favorite people in the world—Exxon executives, Dan Quayle, junk bond salesmen, Millie "The First Dog," Zamfir, master of the pan flute, nuclear power supporters, anyone named Biff, Mr. T, and Jerry Mathers as the "Beaver." Nerts to you,
   Kenneth Cole

Fritz Sands of Woodinville, Washington, is cheesed at:
   George Bush
"Imagine," says Mr. Sands, "a prediction in the summer of 1988 that the president of the United States would, in two years, offer no aid to a Baltic republic attempting to leave the Soviet Union and that he would base that inaction not on risks to the United States but on risks to the political career of Mikhail Gorbachev. Based on this prediction, wouldn't you guess that Walter Mondale, or perhaps Gus Hall, had won the 1988 presidential election?"

Susan G. Gamble of Pittsburgh, Pennsylvania, thumbs her nose at:
   U2 and all other rock groups who claim to speak for anyone other than themselves: U2 sings "Angel of Harlem." What the hell do they know? They're from Ireland.

Paul Castellano of Alexandria, Virginia, is worried about making the punishment fit the crime. He suggests that "all the actors and actresses on the list should be sentenced to five years locked in a screenwriters' seminar. All the weepy-drippy folks who talk about 'networking,' 'spiritual wellness,' etc., should be forced to get a degree—no, make that two degrees—in accounting. And all the television talk show hosts should be forced to adopt lesbian, cross-dressing, obsessive-compulsive children with severe eating disorders."

Geraldine K. Smith of Chichester, New York, writes to remind us of one more hangover from the sixties, the first decade in history to last thirty years:
   Men with long, long hair and earrings

The E. J. Beyer family and their friends—who tell us that they are all over sixty—bring wisdom and experience to bear upon the selection of fools:

Mrs. Betty Ford, for pandering to Planned Parenthood

All those who had a hand in the Alar scare

Pierre Salinger: Why do we have to have *his* insight on news in Europe?

Nelson Mandela, make that St. Mandela, and his not-yet-canonized wife

Edmund Unneland of Jackson Heights, New York, says that he would like "the academic section of our shock troops of the coming *Kulturkampf* to deal with the following":

Arthur Lewin, professor of black studies, who tried to pass off articles in the *Journal of Revolutionary Socialism* as publication deserving of tenure

Joseph Murphy, outgoing leftist chancellor of the City University of New York

Donald Smith, professor of education who attempted to justify a student's assault on a lecturer in physical education by referring to a "white control system"

Middle States Association of Colleges, which deferred accreditation of Baruch College by reason of lower rates of minority student retention

Mr. Unneland goes on to say that the above-named persons and MSAC were "the main elements of the *Putsch* which deposed Joel Segall from the presidency of Baruch College (a part of the City University of New York) for his efforts to resist the establishment of a Black and Hispanic Alumni Association separate from the official group, and for his attempts to establish a test of tenure other than the feather test."

Timothy L. Shell, a graduate student at the University of Florida, lists several Tom Fools:

Daniel Sheehan, head of the Christic Institute: He's not just spreading wild-eyed Iran-contra theories in Washington anymore; now his group has moved to Florida to stop the launch of shuttles carrying nuclear-powered space probes.

Eclipse Comics, which preaches the Christic gospel through the medium of "graphic novels"

Marc Neufeld and Bob Rehme, producers of the upcoming film *Dancin' Cross the River.* This "real-life" drama is based on Daniel Sheehan's legal defense of a black Southern mayor reportedly framed for a crime he didn't commit. The two plan more films about Danny and his kooky Christic cases and causes.

Paramount Pictures, the company that plans to distribute *Dancin' Cross the River*

Ted Danson, who's supposed to play Daniel Sheehan in *Dancin' Cross the River.* Ted also says the world is going to end by 2000.

Black Mountain, North Carolina: Once a beautiful hamlet in the Smoky Mountains, it's now an enclave of peaceniks, crystal-rubbing New Agers, and other primitive life forms.

Martha Plimpton, vegetarian actress who, when asked if she'd kill a cockroach, replied that it's "a question of whether that roach has a real, constructive place on this earth"

Anyone who thinks D.C. statehood is a good idea

Phil Sokolof, the guy who bought those full-page newspaper ads accusing McDonald's of "poisoning" America with its food. [That's *four* McD references in the E-List, readers. An icon, or what?]

The University of Florida Democrats, who showed their unswerving devotion to freedom of speech by trying to shout down Oliver North when he spoke here

Neal D. Bernard, president of Physicians Committee for Responsible Medicine. This clown says, "If you're a meat-eater, you are contributing to the destruction of the environment." Can you imagine if the whole world took his advice? Six billion people subsisting on beans, rice, and corn—the potential methane gas from such a situation is truly frightening.

Whew, Mr. Shell. That's a thesis and a half. We award you your degree.

Robert J. Cihak of Aberdeen, Washington, has a "beef" with some sawbone quacks, the same bunch who irked our anonymous informant at UCLA:

Physicians for Social Responsibility, the docs who advertised all the diseases and injuries that would result if a nuclear bomb somehow exploded over Seattle. And, therefore, everybody should be against nuclear bombs—the ones under the control of free nations, that is.

We suppose it's all a matter of how one feels about Seattle. Ourselves, we like the Boeing plant.

Lawrence Cranberg of Austin, Texas, has a branding iron warming in the fire for:

Gara La Marche, a member of the National Board of the ACLU, who thumbed his nose at Chief Justice Burger for suggesting that copies of the Constitution be put in cereal boxes

The Edna McConnell Clark Foundation, whose agenda is to help the "disadvantaged." To further that agenda, it helped finance the *Prisoners' Self-Help Litigation Manual*—a six-hundred-page tome by jailhouse lawyer:

Daniel E. Manville, distributed free by the:

ACLU National Prison Project, directed by:

Alvin Bronstein

"The McConnell Foundation has, in fact," says Mr. Cranberg, "helped create three new classes of the disadvantaged: federal judges who must deal with innumerable frivolous habeas corpus petitions from jailhouse lawyers; students in our schools, whose funding has been diminished to help support prisoners at the level deemed suitable by the Edna McConnell Clark Foundation; and the hundreds of prisoners who have been killed and wounded in outbreaks of prison violence that accompanied ACLU/Clark-sponsored prison 'reform.' "

Doug Rivers of Warner Robins, Georgia, takes aim at:

Jeff Smith, public television's prattling peacenik Frugal Gourmet.
    Anybody for Native American pudding?

All sportscasters who persist in explaining to us what great human beings those arrogant, coke-tooting, coed-slugging, 7-Eleven-robbing, stereo-stealing college athletes really are

Col. David Hackworth, a media darling you would never have heard of if not for his rambling, paranoid criticisms of the U.S. military and Marxist critique of U.S. foreign policy

Celebrity ex–drug addicts who are given free airtime and publicity to deliver ostensibly anti-drug commercials which wind up conveying that big-time stars use drugs and get away with it

Anybody associated with any movie that has been described as the "best movie ever made about Vietnam"

All congresspersons named Barbara

"The only problem with the New Enemies List," says Urs B. Furrer of Elmsford, New York, "is that . . . we should remember that more than 40 percent of the people voted for 'Little Duke' in 1988. So while I would like to add a few specifics, I would also like to round up the rest of those commie lefties out there":

Judge Sand of New York, for having the nerve to write an opinion that says begging is a form of constitutionally protected free speech

The Peace Dividend

No-growth economists

People who drive slow in the fast lane

Those ungrateful Greeks, who cursed our military presence and now curse us for wanting to leave

Any group that uses "Defense Fund," "Council," or "League" in its name [With, we presume, the exception of the National Security Council, the American League, and Messrs. Osen and Propson's Robert Bork Legal Defense Fund.]

Anyone who thinks Bernhard Goetz should be in jail

Anyone who thinks Michael Milken should be in jail

Anyone who thinks Oliver North should be in jail

Anyone who thinks he has ended an argument by blaming a problem on Ronald Reagan

Paul Kirchner of Hamden, Connecticut, tells us "trying to list the left-wingers in showbiz is like trying to conduct a cockroach census in my old Lower East Side apartment. . . . Wouldn't it be easier to make a special case of Hollywood and list everyone who *isn't* a Commie?" OK, we'll give it a try:

Hollywood Anti-Blacklist Roster of Conservative Heroes and Pals

Arnold Schwarzenegger

Robert Stack

Chuck Norris

Tom Selleck

Charlton Heston

Ricardo Montalban

Jan Michael Vincent

John Milius

Marilyn Chambers: She cruises the annual *Soldier of Fortune* convention, so I guess she's OK.

Sean Connery

Clint Eastwood, though he showed squishy tendencies over there in Cannes

Stallone and George Hamilton: they liked the Marcoses, but does that make them right-wingers?

Anyone who appears in a Bob Hope special

"I haven't investigated Sam Kinison," says Mr. Kirchner, "but he's my hero for saying 'America doesn't have the guts to admit that Whoopi Goldberg isn't funny.'"

Now, back to condemning people to perdition. John D. Kelley of Portland, Maine, gives the bum's rush to:

> *Anyone who actually believes there is a law, either written or implied,*
> *stating that society must support the struggling artist*

Ben Vowels and Randy Brandt of Davis and Ramona, California, respectively, send us a "New Enemies Primer." Herewith some samples therefrom:

> *D is for Dukakis, the political joke*
> *Kitty's in rehab and Massachusetts is broke*

> *N is for Nunn; though not as liberal as Ted*
> *When his interest's at heart, he'll jump right into bed*

> *O is for Ortega, cheered on by Winger*
> *So let's send Debra there, attached to a Stinger*

> *T is for Tutu, spouting ANC baloney*
> *Falwell was right when he called him a phony*

> *X is for Malcolm, a bad dude of old*
> *Now joined by Abbie where it never gets cold*

Donald Whidder, who leaves us to speculate about his address, would give the gate to:

> *All the Palestinian punks who throw rocks in the infantilah (sic)*
> *Oscar Arias Sanchez, appeaser*
> *The City of Miami, except for the Latin Quarter*
> *All codgers who want free medical care but want younger people to pay for it*

Ed Green of Charleston, New York, says,

> It would be too bad if *Dr. Alan Chartock* couldn't be included on your list. He is executive director/producer/fund raiser of our local NPR affiliate WAMC; professor of political science at SUNY New Paltz; professor of communications at SUNY Albany; and political commentator for the local CBS-TV affiliate. On Chartock's weekly half-hour show on WAMC he usually interviews Governor Cuomo and fawns like a court

jester. Much of the time the show is a giggle-fest between the two. I think that Chartock is bucking for press secretary in a Cuomo administration.

It seems to us that between the giggle-fests and the press secretary ambition, life has already punished Dr. Chartock enough.

Mike Avery of Eau Claire, Wisconsin, is strongly opposed to:
acid cut with strychnine
urine tests
Hand Gun Control, Inc.
and—no offense, Mike, but this comes as frankly no surprise—
the Eau Claire Police Department

Mark S. Chmura of Michigan State University wants us to know that Michigan State "is filled with misguided liberal fanatics whose so-called 'minds' are so open that you could fly the Space Shuttle through them."

Robert McWilliams of Phoenix, Arizona, expressing an apposite sentiment in these Husseinish times, shakes bell, book, and candle at:
Anyone who talks about the "Three Great Faiths of the World, Islam,
Christianity, and Judaism": Those who talk like this about Islam
sound strangely like those who once gushed about communism. Has
the left found a new idol to adore?

Lieutenant Mark G. Martin of San Diego, California, showing an officer's proper concern for his men, damns:
Government officials who give Nicaragua millions but won't pay enlisted
U.S. military personnel a living wage

Theodore A. Bundesen of San Jose, California, says, "The following flap-doodlers, featherbrains, and freeloaders are alarmingly absent from your list":
The San Mateo Lincoln Club, known locally as the "Kennedy Klub,"
which promotes Republican candidates so liberal they would run as
Democrats if the Democratic party didn't insist they wear sandals
The U.S. Justice Department: Now that RICO laws have voided the
Constitution, this leftist lawyer-employment agency is targeting people
for "eco-crimes." Thought crimes can't be far off.
The northern spotted owl: hardly worth the barbecue sauce

George Bush (reluctantly): Hey, George, do you remember the oath of
   office? It charges you with protecting the Constitution. That's what the
   veto is for. It's pretty simple: if Congress passes it, you veto it.
We note here the third George Bush excommunication in this Enemies List and
suggest that, if this keeps up, the president may want to do his future fund-raising
over at People for the American Way.

L arry A. Wilke of St. Louis, Missouri, gives a back of the hand from the
  heartland to:
   Anyone who uses the "misery index"
   Anyone who thought it important to put girls in the Boy Scouts
   Believers in the "invisible poor"
   Believers in the "feminization of poverty"
   Believers in "Iranian moderates"
   Animal psychologists
   The Twenty-Second Amendment

Charles E. Krakoff, who's been living in Africa for the past couple of years,
sends us a sub-Saharan edition of the E-List:
   Julius Nyerere, Africa's top Stalinist, at least until Mengistu came along.
      He has probably killed more people than Idi Amin or Bokassa, even if
      he didn't eat them.
   Kenneth Kaunda: Just imagine that you were put in charge of the richest
      country in Africa at the time, and instructed to ruin it as completely
      and quickly as possible; you couldn't do better than KK has in twenty-
      five short years.
   Mobutu Sese Seko: Okay, he's supposed to be one of our friends, but he has
      stolen enough from his country to make Marcos look like a petty thief.

Paul A. Pangallo of Indianapolis, Indiana, returns us to more familiar territory,
throwing cold water upon:
   The people who held hands and stood on a hillside and sang the Coca-Cola song

Our penultimate correspondent, R. S. Bearse of Arlington, Virginia, where
many of our best informants—and we ourselves—seem to come from, calls
down the lightning upon:
   *Those who didn't get goosebumps every time President Reagan said,
      "God bless you and God bless America"*

And, last of all, we have an Enemies List entry I'll bet none of you included: Nathan A. Forney of Rockwood, Illinois, explains that the "For Women Only" column in the Fall 1988 issue of *Spinal Cord Injury Life* announced to the world the founding of a newsletter called—and he's not pulling our prosthetic device, he sent the clipping to prove it—

Dykes, Disability and Stuff

With that we bid you adieu. *Semper fi.* And don't forget, the Commie you clobber may be—whoops—your own dim-bulb, teenage, Grateful Dead–fan kid. ❖

≪ V ≫

Insult the
Injured

The American Spectator, November 1991

springs

This installment of the Enemies List is about a quart low on yellow bile. Which is nothing to be ashamed of. Conservatism is not a vulgar mass movement that needs to foster hatred as a "unifying agent." Nor are we, like the jejune progressives, angry because established things are established and we are not. We rule the world. Ha ha. And cheerfully. Yes, we can afford to be indulgent toward the *left*-outs and the *left*-overs and their ever more pathetic fantasies of influence and power. But that's not why this list is relatively short. We can afford to be indulgent, but we aren't. The bullying communard palaver spewed by fascist Levelers is as repulsive now as it was when it had a Soviet army attached to it. We loathe these intellectual gulagmongers as much as we ever did. We still want them marched north onto the pack ice of Hudson's Bay and there, clad only in Birkenstock sandals, set to the task of teaching polar bears vegetarianism. We're conservatives. We know evil exists. And we're able and willing to identify it in that long police lineup which is modern politics. But there's the problem. This is the fifth Enemies List. Evildoers with any kind of public name, we've publicly named them. We're beginning to repeat ourselves or belabor the obvious: the Kennedy family and their never-ending zipper problems, Winnie Mandela with her Leon Spinks approach to political indoctrination of the young, Molly Yard, Senator Paul Wellstone, Saddam Hussein, Ann Richards, Kitty Kelley, David Dinkins, Linda Ellerbee, Linda Ellerbee, Linda Ellerbee.

There's some value, of course, to reiterated denunciations. It would be hard to put Sinead O'Connor on an enemies list too many times. She *is* the entire left-wing thought process: "The world faces difficult and horrendous problems—war, famine, disease, poverty, and injustice. We could ask scientists and scholars what to do about these problems or pray to God for guidance, or we could study the problems ourselves and try to discern solutions, but fortunately, we don't have to do any of that because there's a bald girl in Dublin who has all the answers." Worthy though such duplication is, however, it's boring. And to be boring violates the first rule of retribution: "If it's boring it isn't really revenge."

Speaking of revenge, we still have not, even after years of trying, invented a suitable means of blackening the fates of our blacklistees. I have two more suggestions:

Smoke. Smoke cigarettes, smoke pipes, but especially smoke cigars, the great big capitalist-pig chair-leg-sized stogies that smell like barbecuing snow tires. Smoking probably isn't very good for us, but it drives liberals mad, propels them into frenzies of indignation and sanctimoniousness. They flop around in paroxysms or worry about the effects of passive smoke inhalation. It's a well-known fact that every year thousands of liberals die from having fits about staying healthy.

Shoot cats. Why lefties have such a pronounced affinity for these dislikable, useless, and eminently unendangered knaves of the animal kingdom is no mystery. Cats are disloyal, self-regarding layabouts with nothing but contempt for those who feed and protect them. Left-wingers acknowledge this likeness by giving cats names such as "Che," "Chairman Meow," and "Linda Ellerbee." Owning a cat is as close as most pinkos come to having a normal personal relationship. (I had no more penned these words than, opening the September 9 *International Herald Tribune*, I was confronted by a five-column review of a New Age self-awareness book titled *Know Yourself Through Your Cat*. The obviously insane author, Vivienne Angus, said: "I'm a great believer that in everybody is every animal and every animal is in everybody." Shoot cats, *Q.E.D.)*

Another reason why this Enemies List is a tad brief is that other people have taken up the idea and even improved upon it. Thank you, Boris Yeltsin. We've got a call in to Boris, and we hope soon to have all U.S. "Soviet experts" —Stephen F. Cohen first among them—indicted with the rest of the coup conspirators. Also, now that the KGB is on our side, expect Lawrence Walsh to have a mysterious accident in the bath. Another fine job is being done by L. Brent Bozell III. We may have named Cranston, Biden, and Kennedy here first, but it was Brent who ponied up for the TV ads. However, the best post-*American Spectator* proscription is Don Kowet's "Desert Storm Hall of Shame," which ran daily in the *Washington Times*'s Life section for three weeks last March and named and quoted more than two dozen Persian Gulf peace creeps. Herewith, a Hall of Shame sampler:

Dreadful *New York Times* columnist *Anna Quindlen:* "Can we live as a country with the knowledge that once again the children of the poor and of people of color will be killed for the convictions of well-to-do white men?"

Appalling *Washington Post* columnist *Colman McCarthy:* "The reason for not supporting U.S. troops was the same for not supporting Iraqi troops, or any troops anywhere for any reason. They are anti-life."

Pantsless pot-walloper *Ted Kennedy:* "We're talking about the likelihood of at least 3,000 American casualties a week, with 700 dead, for as long as the war goes on."

Actual socialist—live and in captivity—*Bernie Sanders:* "Is [a ground war] worth 30,000 or 40,000 casualties? The figures that I have stated come from the Center for Defense [Dis]Information, Admiral La Rocque's group. I think they have a fairly good reputation."

Congressional bucket-mouth *James Traficant, Jr.:* "Why did the Pentagon recently order 16,000 human remains pouches?"

Overrated novelist *E. L. Doctorow:* "There is a rumor going about that . . . the Quartermaster Corps of the Army has ordered 80,000 body bags."

World's wettest former Secretary of the Navy *James Webb:* "Does anybody really believe that we can launch an attack in January, then secure, occupy, and stabilize Kuwait and withdraw from Saudi Arabia by March?"

Noted troglodyte *Pat Buchanan:* "What could the United States do, should Iraq overrun Kuwait? With a battle-hardened army larger than our own, Iraq could not be stopped on the ground."

Stupid Senator *Bob Kerrey:* "We should tell [Saddam Hussein] we are not going to declare war and will not initiate attack under the current circumstances."

Stupid and vile Senator *John Kerry:* "Are we ready for the changes this war will bring—changes in sons and daughters who return from combat never the same, some not knowing their families and their families not even recognizing them?"

And a special combination partial plate and wing-tip oxford to the chief dim-bulb at the Center for Strategic and International Studies, *Edward N. Luttwak:* "I don't think there will be a land war. . . . If war does break out, there is the possibility of an ignominious [U.S.] debacle. . . . If there is a U.S. ground offensive of any size, the resulting casualties could easily destroy the Bush presidency, regardless of whatever victories are won. . . . The Iraqis are too combat-experienced to run away under fire. . . . The [U.S.] Army's armored and mechanized forces can play no offensive role against the vast defensive strength of the Iraqi army."

N ow for our own list. Donald Rizzi of Alameda, California, kicks off with boot toe put to:

Any college or university that gives up its Indian nickname and then wonders why many alumni stop sending wampum

W. Austerman of San Antonio, Texas, lets fly with a roundhouse right at:

The lamebrained CBS newscaster of October 7, 1990, who blamed "capitalism and greed" for another abysmal harvest in the USSR
President George Bush who forgot (if he ever knew) Napoleon Bonaparte's eminently sensible dictum, "If you decide to take Vienna, THEN TAKE VIENNA!"

Michael Wright of Redondo Beach, California, gives a Dutch rub and a noogie to:

Republicans who campaign as bulwarks against liberal fabulism and who, upon election, double over and do 95 percent of what their opponents would do. For example,
George Bush, for betting the farm on Gorbachev, the Rostenkowski tax hike, and conditional acceptance of gun control as appended to the Bush crime bill

    Pete Wilson, for appointing Sierra Clubbers to high state posts, for
        appointing John Seymour to the U.S. Senate, and for generally
        keeping the flame of Lowell Weicker alive
    John Seymour, for voting for the Democrats' pet gun-ban bill as a
        California state senator, and supporting more of the same in Washington

Bill Glenn of Kamiah, Idaho, sends along, as wrapping on a brickbat, a painstakingly fair newspaper profile of a young man who calls himself *KRS-One*. Mr. One is, it seems, a respected professional in the rap song industry, and it is his considered belief that the American flag is worse than a swastika, that the American government has been trying to control population growth through AIDS and crack cocaine, and that Abraham Lincoln introduced capitalism to America. Mr. One delivered himself of these philosophical insights at the *University of Idaho*, where the audience gave him a standing ovation.

Mary A. Lane of Seattle, Washington, swats with a large paddle:
    Writers of European travel books who warn their readers not to be Ugly
        Americans

An anonymous well-wisher of no fixed address turns hungry Rottweilers loose upon:
    Any spondaic, dactylic, or anapestic feminist book titles:
        (1) Men Who Love Women and the Children They Bear
        (2) Fat Is a Feminist Issue
        (3) Women Who Love Too Much
        (4) Smart Women, Foolish Choices
    Hedrick Smith, who consistently uses liberal doublespeak and calls hard-
        core Soviet Communist gerontocrats "The Right"
    "The American Agenda" segments on ABC News: The producers should
        be a little disingenuous and call them "The Liberal Agenda."
    Republicans who feel it's time to "govern"
    Reporters and commentators who use the words "courage," "wisdom," or
        "making tough choices" as disguised synonyms for "willingness to tax"

Nick Renton and John Schroeder or Los Angeles, California, give a poke in the eye, Moe Stooge–style, to anybody who:
    uses the word "diversity" and isn't referring to a stock portfolio
    says "herstory" (she should be given an immediate herstorectomy)
    capitalizes the word "green"
    worships goddesses

thinks Egyptians were black
is still whining about the Willie Horton ad

Debbie Melman, also from out California way, will be backing her car in and out of handicapped parking spaces, hoping to run over:
Differently Abled Dykes
Anybody who is "thinking globally and acting locally"
Any man who hasn't chuckled at least once over the Zeke Mowatt affair

Gary Malmberg of St. Paul, Minnesota, wishes a Michael Milken–led hostile takeover would descend on:
Sharp Electronics: They ran anti-Reagan ads in the U.K.
Toyota: Their spokesman is Martin Sheen.

Jennifer and Mike Durham of Raleigh, North Carolina, have in their cross-hair sights:
Anyone claiming membership in an organization whose name contains one or more of the following: "against," "coalition," "social," "peace," "offensive," "ethical," "world," "action," "friends of," "environment," "unity"

Charity begins at home, not on Mars, says C. K. Taylor of Washington, D.C., who would like to see the *Combined Federal Campaign* permanently deducted from life, "for attempting to wrest donations from federal workers at the same time they were threatened with furlough, but more importantly for including the following as charities":
Shoe and Rubber Fund, D.C. Congress of Parents and Teachers: "provides tennis, leather shoes and boots to District of Columbia public school children." (I'll bet you thought we were talking condoms.)
The Divine Universal Sisterhood, Inc.
Bonabond, Inc.: "provides supervision for persons who cannot afford or qualify for personal recognizance release"
Feminist Institute, Inc.: "promotes social justice and feminist social change through national clearinghouse, research, education, and change projects; violence prevention, feminist tours, feminist camp; aging, and other projects"
Sexual Minority Youth Assistance League (SMYAL), Inc.: "SMYAL is a youth social services and advocacy agency that seeks to prevent the abuse, neglect, and self-hatred of gay, lesbian, and bisexual youth."

Burning books is wrong, but there's nothing the matter with setting fire to an occasional librarian. Keith Coffman of Westminster, Colorado, has his Zippo ready and is waiting outside:

> *The Boulder, Colorado, public library:* for banning the Hardy Boys detective series from its shelves

From C. H. Ross of Nashville, Tennessee, one apple (with Ninja worm) to:

> *The National Education Association*: If you can read this, don't thank one of these teachers.

Adrian H. Krieg of Acworth, New York, wishes all manner of natural ills upon:

> *Rachel Carson:* She published *The Silent Spring* in 1962, predicting the end of the world in twenty years.
> *Paul Ehrlich:* He published *The Population Bomb* in 1967, predicting starvation and overpopulation by 1980.
> *George Wald:* In 1975 he predicted the end of the world by 1985 due to political problems.
> *Rene Dubos:* In 1972 he predicted the end of the world by 1997 due to overindustrialization.

And Paul H. Liben of Yonkers, New York, sends us a big, big, big Linda Ellerbee of a letter, all handwritten. Frankly, Mr. Liben, your handwriting is almost as incomprehensible as the political beliefs of the people you are indicting. But we did manage to pick this item from among your 158 Enemies List nominations:

> *Liberal clergymen who wear traditional wool suits from Brooks Brothers*

This brings us to a huge and amazing pile of stuff that has been accumulating in our office for nearly a year. An anonymous correspondent in the San Francisco area has been collecting all the posters, handbills, flyers, and so forth that appear in such profusion in Berkeley, Oakland, and the other captive nations of the East Bay region. Thus our correspondent shows him or herself to be a committed environmentalist—providing us with a rich compost of enemy listings and fighting litter at the same time. Here are just a few of the organizations that have been killing trees and wasting recycled paper to make themselves ridiculous in print:

> *500 Years of Resistance Committee*
> *Church of Peace and Plenty*

Earth Drama Lab
Pesticide Action Network
San Francisco League of Urban Gardeners
Sea Turtle Restoration Project
Friends of American Medical Relief Comm. in the West Bank and Gaza
Food Not Bombs
Middle East Children's Alliance
Roots Against War
Samoans for Samoans of California
San Francisco Mime Troupe
Santa Cruz Christic Action Team
Students Against U.S. Intervention in the Gulf at San Francisco State
    University
National Association of Black and White Men Together
Tenderloin Self-Help Center
U.S.-Vietnam Friendship Association
Women Against Imperialism
Alliance for Philippine Concerns
Patrice Lumumba Coalition
Bring the Frigates Home Coalition, Sydney, Australia
Committee for Peace and Reunification in Korea
Dominican Workers Party
Committee vs. Repression in Haiti
Tyne Daly
Spike Lee
Committee for Puerto Rican Affirmation
Mozambique Support Network
National Coalition vs. English Only
Nipmuc Indian Nation Warriors Society, Boston
Palm Beach Coalition for World Peace
Daughters of Mother Jones
Art Against the War
Hands Off Cuba [Yes, the very same for which Lee Harvey Oswald
    toiled so long and hard.]
And here's one that is just about impossible to top:
Lesbians in Solidarity with the Palestinian People

Among the riper examples of literature from the above ilk, we have an ad that reads: "Censored Video: See Former U.S. Attorney General Ramsey Clark's

Recent Trip Through the Iraq War Zone." (How smart can our smart bombs be if they missed him?) And a dreary, tendentious newspaper called *Street Sheet,* which sells for a dollar and says of itself: "We are presently providing 50 papers a weekday to over 30 [homeless] people at absolutely no cost to them." (You may have wondered how the homeless could revel every night midst the glitter of downtown while the rest of us can barely afford to go out once a week.)

We also have a screed from *Women Organizing for Social and Economic Justice,* touting their "Movements for Justice Panel Series." The heck with the Easter ski trip, this is a definite must-see:

> ## WOMEN OF COLOR AND
> ## REPRODUCTIVE RIGHTS
> Saturday, March 23, 1:00–2:30
>
> How do women of color develop strategic
> plans around AIDS, the health care delivery system,
> sex/health education programs, teen pregnancy,
> reproductive safety in the workplace, abortion,
> and other reproductive issues particular to us? How
> can we put our struggles for reproductive rights both
> on the agendas of the larger reproductive rights
> movement and on the agendas of labor and
> community-based organizations of color?

Then there's the *End French Testing in Tahiti* poster, and another poster depicting the adventures of a superhero named *BleachMan.* This caped crusader urges drug addicts to rinse their syringes in his namesake and avoid AIDS. A great Halloween outfit for the kids.

It's hard to pick the best-of-show here. Certainly the handbill for the *Gay and Lesbian Leather Community*'s benefit beer blast with "Leather Erotica Raffle" is a contender. As is the mailer for the gay bar that offers, on alternate Saturdays, "Basement Bondage Party" and "Green Party," where one can "Meet the Rainforest Action Network." Then there's the *Office Workers United*'s printed plea to "shut down the Pacific Stock Exchange":

On Monday the 29th . . .
1. Join us (in costume if you like) in actually shutting down the stock
   exchange itself (301 Pine Street at Sansome).

2. Use the general disruption as an excuse to arrive (very) late at work.
3. Call in sick (of capitalist exploitation and environmental destruction).

DEFEND THE EARTH! DEFEND YOUR RIGHTS!
EARTH AND PEOPLE BEFORE PROFITS!

And a flyer advertising *Pasta for Peace in El Salvador* pushes the envelope of human silliness. Or you think it does until you read this astonishing statement from the *People's Democratic Uhuru Movement:*

> Representing the interests of the African working class movement inside the borders of the U.S., the People's Democratic Uhuru Movement is the only voice raising up the fact that the land and the oil belong to the Arab people! . . . The PDUM calls for Victory to Iraq and solidarity with the Arab people. But we must go farther than this.
>
> For African and colonized people in this country a full-scale U.S. war is already aimed at us! We already live in bombed out, burned out communities and experience the brunt of total martial law which comes down on us currently under the guise of the so-called "war on drugs." While we stand up against U.S. aggression on Iraq, we have to stand up against the all-out counterinsurgency being waged against African people.
>
> Everybody knows that "The White House is the Rock House" and "Uncle Sam is the Pusherman." . . .

But, in the end, we must award the grand prize shut-up kudos to the campaign literature of one Gloria La Riva, who is running for mayor of San Francisco on the idiot ticket. Ms. Riva—earnest, pudgy, and gaping in her photograph—is introduced to the voters thus:

> You may know Gloria as one of the spokespersons and a tireless activist in the Emergency Committee to Stop the U.S. War in the Middle East. Or as an initiator of the Farmworkers Emergency Relief effort. Or as a candidate for Mayor in 1983, when she finished third, and in second place in many working class neighborhoods; including the Mission, Fillmore, Castro, and Haight.
>
> You may be familiar with Gloria as a leader of the All People's Congress, fighting the proposed baseball stadium or the MUNI fare increases, fighting for expanded aid to victims of the earthquake or supporting the fight of Black firefighters for affirmative action. Perhaps

you have met her in solidarity work for South Africa, Palestine, or Central America.

Whew! First wife from hell.

Now let us complete this Enemies List with a few acts of Christian Charity. C. H. Ross, who earlier in this chapter condemned the NEA, has decided to let the Pope off with a warning:
> *Pope John Paul II* is hereby reprieved on account of the encyclical *Centesimus Annus*. I have notified him, however, that he remains on strict probation.

And Gary Osen and Thomas Propson of Washington, D.C., seem to be conducting a regular love-in. But, gosh, we're only on this planet once, so let's heed Gary and Tom's example and try to make it a little nicer place. "Last year we made our contribution to freedom by naming some of its chronic abusers. This year we would like to suggest that a place be set aside amongst the 'Guilty by Suspicion' for those recidivists who, in the great liberal tradition, deserve a one-year furlough":
> *Saddam Hussein:* Ordinarily, bloodthirsty despots do not ingratiate themselves by using poison gas on defenseless civilians, invading weak neighbors, and setting fire to our precious bubbly. However, some credit has to be given to a world leader willing to stand up to the environmental movement.
> *The Republican Guard:* Inept, murderous, and mostly dead—but aptly named. They have done a hell of a lot more to guard Republicans in '92 than either Messrs. Darman or Sununu.
> *Saudi Arabia:* It may be a barren, desolate hellhole kept afloat by American technology, Bangladeshi workers, and German automobiles, but if it makes Molly Yard indignant it's sure as heck worth dying for!
> *ACT UP:* While we are not normally fond of militant homosexual groups that harass the Catholic Church and, even more sacrilegiously, disrupt the stock market, we feel that amnesty must be granted to anyone who manages to get Dan Rather off the air—even for five minutes.
> *The National Enquirer:* They fabricate, defame, slander and publicize the perversions, depravity, and moral decadence of half-wit, substance-abusing entertainers—but now they're doing it to the Kennedy clan! ❖

⪻ VI ⪼

Commies— Dead but Too Dumb to Lie Down

The American Spectator, November 1992

This year: dirty-money groups and individuals who fund neo-, proto-, crypto-, demi-, semi-, and plain Ben & Jerry's vanilla Communism in the United States—plus the special "Peter Ueberroth Gold Medal for 100-Meter-Dash-Carrying-a-VCR" awards to those who did the most to provide L.A. murderers and thieves with moral, political, and philosophic justification for all the fun they had.

Let us commence without preamble what that unmourned sixties radical Danny the (Now Better Than) Red called "The Long March Through the Institutions."

We have two Supercontributors to this Enemies List. First, there is the lovely (ah, the joys of being a middle-aged Republican and thus allowed to compliment the ladies with a clear conscience and, even, a twinkling eye) Kimberly O. Dennis. Ms. Dennis is the executive director of the Philanthropy Roundtable, an organization that promotes the astonishing idea that charity ought to help people (320 N. Meridian St., Indianapolis, IN 46204, in case you'd like to make a donation). Ms. Dennis directs our attention to the Philadelphia-based *Pew Charitable Trusts*. Founded by the owners of Sun Oil and once a model group of charities giving money to churches, schools, museums, homes for the retarded, and other such worthy causes, the Pew Trusts have come down with Ford Foundation Syndrome. A diseased itch for social engineering has replaced a healthy instinct for social service. According to the April 26, 1992, edition of the *Philadelphia Inquirer*:

> Instead of continuing to fund neighborhood centers to help poor people with their heating bills, Pew gave $5 million in a joint effort with three other big foundations to set up an Energy Foundation to provide grants to promote energy efficiency.
>
> Instead of expanding local child-welfare programs, Pew gave $2.5 million to a New York research corporation to develop a demonstration project "to improve the earnings of absent fathers, the effectiveness of the child-support enforcement system and the financial well-being of poor children."

You get the picture.

Foundation News, one of the hand-out industry's professional journals, crowed that the Pew Charitable Trusts "eliminated almost all of their right-wing grantmaking and embraced a broad range of projects, including some that manifestly oppose the business interests the old Pews held inviolable." In other words, the Pew trustees haven't actually killed the golden goose but they *are* chasing it around the yard with an axe.

Of course, no one suffers from Ford Foundation Syndrome like the *Ford Foundation*, which has in the past done the nation such favors as underwriting public television, creating pilot programs for LBJ's "War on Poverty," and providing post-assassination grants to Robert F. Kennedy's staff to help them overcome their grief.

Ms. Dennis sends us a package of information on the Ford Foundation's current activities. Ford is paying to create "advocacy centers" for children in Nigeria—not giving them food or health care, mind you, but giving them a place to make complaints about the lack thereof. Ford is "explor[ing] the obstacles to settling the Palestinian-Israeli conflict"—expecting a few New York double domes to accomplish with one study grant what God Himself has not been able to do in five thousand years. And Ford is testing Norplant birth-control devices on Bangladeshi women. Which sounds not only genocidal but also counterproductive: What's the Ford Foundation going to do with itself if it doesn't have lots of impoverished Third Worlders to pester and bully?

Ms. Dennis also re-alerts us to the activities of the damnable *MacArthur Foundation* (vivisected by our own Joshua Muravchik in the January 1992 *American Spectator*). There's been another Big Mac Attack, with so-called genius grants being punted to the likes of:

> Janet Benshoof, 45, New York, president of the Center for Reproductive Law and Policy and a litigator and educator in the areas of abortion rights and contraception, awarded $280,000

> Evelyn Fox Keller, professor at University of California, Berkeley, [who] analyzed the social construction of science and the role of sex in how science is conducted, $335,000

> Paule Marshall, 63, Richmond, Va., professor at Virginia Commonwealth University, writer whose fiction explores healing divided selves, divided cultures, and a divided world, $369,000

> John Terborgh, 56, Durham, N.C., director of Duke University Center for Tropical Conservation, biologist working in ecology, biogeography, biological conservation and training Peruvian conservation biologists, $335,000

Training them to duck, we hope.

And, finally, Ms. Dennis sends us an issue of the Roundtable's quarterly publication, *Philanthropy*, in which the United Way scandal is analyzed and the abuses of its former president William Aramony are shown to be "simply the most visible manifestation of the organization's growing immoderation and ambition." The article's author, chairman of the Philanthropy Roundtable Michael S. Joyce, goes on to say:

> United Way of America . . . provides staff training and development, promotes United Way nationally, and lobbies federal and state law-makers to support public policy initiatives on literacy, homelessness, drug abuse, and other social issues. [Donors may wonder why their contributions are being used to lobby the government to supply the services United Way is meant to render.] To the extent United Way controls the flow of multitudinous individual donations, groups are forced to meet the agency's specifications in order to maintain their funding. If United Way says it will only support the Boy Scouts if it allows girls or homosexuals or atheists to be members, the Boy Scouts either have to comply or lose access to the masses of donations that are channeled through the agency.

Our second Enemies List megasource is Willa Ann Johnson, founder and chairman of the Capital Research Center (1612 K St., NW, Suite 704, Washington, DC 20006). This fine organization, in Ms. Johnson's own words,

> was formed to provide positive new alternatives to the hitherto-dominant culture of philanthropy in America. By challenging the progressive ideology of the public interest culture, Capital Research is helping the philanthropic community rediscover the bedrock principles of individual initiative and responsibility in a free society.

Ms. Johnson writes us a letter saying:

> I have learned from John Von Kannon that you have begun work on your new "Enemies List." . . . I am emboldened to submit the following organizations: The Council on Foundations, Campaign for Human Development, National Organization for Women, Alliance for Justice, AARP, League of Women Voters, Center for Science in the Public Interest, Children's Defense Fund, and Greenpeace.

She encloses a massive package of research material. Herewith, some extracts.

Of the *Council on Foundations*, Capital Research Center senior fellow Marvin Olasky writes:

To the Chicago Hilton on April 22 [1991] came 2,000 foundation
executives and staff members for the 42nd annual conference of the
Council on Foundations. . . . I have been following the Council on
Foundations, and tracking the $3,600,000 in annual giving its 1,200
members control, since 1985.

Mr. Olasky then details conference sessions and panels on such topics as:

"Task Force on Inclusiveness"—to help COF members adapt to "the
new pluralism"
"Reproductive Rights Breakfast Roundtable" [Yum, say the editors.]
"Civil Rights in the 1990s"
"Civil Disobedience in the Civil Society"—with one panelist saying, "We
live in a time of terrible somnolence and anesthesia . . ."
"Marketing Our Good Work"—"proactively going after media attention"
"Working Group on Funding Lesbian and Gay Issues"
"Culture and Community Empowerment"—led by one Jane Sapp, director
of the Center for Cultural Community Development at Springfield
College in Massachusetts, who said: "I wish I could have had this
conversation back in 1492. . . . If we had sat down in 1492 and said,
'How do we begin to find a way for all of us to talk together about who
we are,' we would not have had today's problems. . . . The word is
domination. . . . You took away the music . . . you took away self-esteem
. . . you made me a consumer."

Poor Mr. Olasky also attends the conference's film festival, where he views
such artistic triumphs as:

Berkeley in the Sixties
Global Dumping Ground—"America's dirty secret . . . export of toxic
waste"
Borderline Medicine—praising Canada's national health insurance
H-2 Worker—substandard living and working conditions in the sugar
cane industry
Streetlife: *The Invisible Family*
Amazonia: Voices from the Rainforest and Chemical Valley—set in West
Virginia and funded by the Ford Foundation, the National Endowment
for the Arts, etc., and containing such memorable lines as "They killed
the Indians, now they're killing the hillbillies."

The *Campaign for Human Development* is one of the Catholic Church's largest
charitable programs. It's run by the U.S. Catholic Conference under the auspices of

the National Conference of Bishops. In 1990 CHD raised $9.82 million. Here's what some of that money goes for:

> Expanding Communications to Empower Indian People of Fort Bethold ($33,000) . . . Amnesty Farmworkers Organizing Project ($25,000) . . . Build Homes Not Bombs ($20,000) . . . Virginia Association Against the Death Penalty ($30,000) . . . Organizing and Educating for Legislative Advocacy on Welfare Issues ($30,000) . . . Parents United for Child Care ($40,000) . . . Campaign for Accessible Health Care ($40,000) . . . and the Association of Community Organizations for Reform Now (ACORN), a product of 1960s radical activism that engages in community organizing to "win the maximum amount of political power possible to be exercised by our constituency and their organization." The goal: "for low-to-moderate income people to take back what's rightfully ours," which, to ACORN, means "everything." Between 1978 and 1989 CHD funneled better than $1,000,000 to ACORN projects across the United States.

The *Alliance for Justice* is headed by Nan Aron, formerly of the horrible ACLU. Says the Capital Research Center:

> Alliance . . . is an amalgam of groups that took a leadership role in lobbying against confirmation of Robert Bork and Clarence Thomas to the Supreme Court. It also opposed confirmation of Justice David Souter, spearheaded the successful fight against Judge Kenneth Ryskamp's nomination to the Eleventh Circuit Court of Appeals, and was critical of the nomination of Kenneth Starr to be Solicitor General because of his allegedly "restrictive views on the role of the courts" and presumed "insensitivity to the rights of minorities." . . . According to the *New York Times*, it was officials of the Alliance for Justice who first brought Anita Hill to the Senate Judiciary Committee's attention.

The *League of Women Voters* is about as nonpartisan as the House of Representatives. Capital Research Center notes that the League

> supports increased welfare spending . . . while opposing increases in the defense budget. . . . The League says it "will be working to ensure that the federal government has overall responsibility for financing basic income-assistance programs." . . . The League opposed "enactment [in 1985] of the Gramm-Rudman-Hollings Balanced Budget and Emergency Deficit Control Act" . . . and also opposes both the so-called "line-item veto" (at

the federal level) and "a proposed constitutional amendment mandating a balanced budget." . . .

[The League opposed] "efforts to substitute private programs for social   security." The League also "opposes any initiatives that would reduce   social security benefits to achieve deficit reductions."

. . . The League supports "clean-air" legislation that would "institute a tough acid-rain control program." . . .

The League of Women Voters is listed in the "peace" movement–oriented *Peace Resource Book: A Comprehensive Guide to Issues, Groups, and Literature, 1986,* which describes the League as a women's "Activist Group" which "lobbies against the MX [missile], Star Wars, and increased military spending." . . .

A statement of the League's position on U.S. relations with developing countries announced . . . that "U.S. policies toward developing countries should not be based on maintaining U.S. preeminence for fighting communism."

And—E-Listers take note—"the League condemns the so-called 'witch-hunt' period of the early fifties."

The *Center for Science in the Public Interest* is a Naderite front group. Capital Research points out that CSPI is

> pro-government, pro-tax, pro-regulation, and anti-business. . . . It wants the Department of Agriculture's labeling regulations for meat and poultry, as well as its policy on health claims, to conform to those of the Food and Drug Administration. . . . CSPI's promotion of tougher labeling laws . . . is part of a much larger campaign against the very notion of marketing.

The federal government, says CSPI Director of Legal Affairs Bruce Silverglade, must "put a stop to this marketplace free-for-all." Funding for these nasty little fascists of the supermarket aisles comes from:

S. H. Cowell Foundation ($37,500)
C. S. Fund ($30,000)
Glen Eagles Foundation ($20,000)
George Gund Foundation ($20,000)
Ruth Mott Fund ($50,000)
Wallace Genetic Foundation ($15,000)

The *Children's Defense Fund* is another lovely charity, dear to the heart of Hillary Clinton, no doubt. CDF cares, cares, cares about kids—though not enough to defend them in a war. The Capital Research Center tells us:

At least since the Vietnam War, there has been a growing emphasis within the political left on so-called "economic conversion": taking tax dollars traditionally allocated to national defense and using them instead to underwrite expanded federal involvement in such domestic areas as the environment, health care, and welfare. The Children's Defense Fund, widely perceived simply as a Washington-based children's advocacy group, is a significant part of this movement.

CRC further notes that the 1986 *Peace Resource Book* "describes CDF as a 'Lobby Group' focused on 'Military Spending.'" Among the self-described altruists sponsoring this nonsense:

> *Ford Foundation* (total of $1,000,000)
> *General Mills Foundation* ($10,000)
> *Prudential Foundation* ($10,000)
> *Rockefeller Foundation* ($500,000)
> *Helena Rubenstein Foundation* (total of $55,000)

We have no room here to do justice to the Capital Research Center's work on *Greenpeace*. Let us simply quote from a Greenpeace brochure—"Humanity is not the center of life on the planet. Ecology has taught us that the whole earth is part of our 'body'"—and leave it to the imagination what part of that body Greenpeace has its head up.

Ms. Johnson also sends us a book, *Patterns of Corporate Philanthropy*, by the afore-cited Marvin Olasky with the assistance of Daniel T. Oliver and Robert V. Pambianco. *Patterns* is a detailed account of U.S. corporate charity, and in its pages we find the *Dayton Hudson Corporation* giving money to the Ms. Foundation for Women and the NOW Legal Defense and Education Fund; *General Mills* giving to the Gray Panthers Project Fund, the American Friends Service Committee, and the Minnesota Civil Liberties Union Foundation; *American Express* giving to the Children's Defense Fund and the Women's Action Alliance; and *J. P. Morgan and Company*, of all people, giving to the ACLU. Lenin believed that capitalists would sell him the rope they'd be hanged with. Wrong. They want to give it away free.

Besides the white knights at the Capital Research Center and the Philanthropy Roundtable, countless other readers have been responding to our call to "Arms Not Alms." We can mention only a few score of these patriots.

An anonymous (and, let us hope, unincarcerated) correspondent sends us a note saying: "The *Edna McConnell Clark Foundation* is *the* most active foundation in prison reform. Only their reforms—not!" He or she encloses a Clark

Foundation brochure containing such gems as: "Fear of crime, rather than crime itself, seems to be fueling the nation's rising incarceration rates."

Frank J. O'Neill of Dunlap, California, writes:

> If you have the nerve to join me I would like to nominate one of America's most sacred cows—the *American Association of Retired Persons*. This organization has an operating budget of over $300 million a year, and its policies and lobbying positions go virtually unchallenged by anyone. I submit that there are millions of Americans (many or most of them elderly) that are being subjected to the liberal line of propaganda through *Modern Maturity* magazine and the *AARP Bulletin*.

He sends along a copy of the July-August 1992 *AARP Bulletin*, with a lead article showing how well pink and gray go together:

> No sooner did Lovola Burgess take over as AARP's new president than she vigorously defended older Americans against charges they are diverting resources away from children in need.
> "To think, as some people do, that programs like Social Security and Medicare are the cause of the growing rate of poverty among children is wrong," Burgess said. "Utterly wrong."
> "The issue isn't old versus young," she added. "It's the 'haves' versus the 'have nots' in our society."

Mark A. Siefert of Muskego, Wisconsin, says what he'd like to do to com-symps is nail their bleeding hearts to the door of every college building in the U.S. "But, since we have laws, religion, and morality, we have to make do with the New Enemies List." He proposes for effigy portal-spiking:
Esprit de Corps, for its "What would you do to change the world" ads, which glorify gun control, abortion, and Afrocentrism
Levi Strauss, for cutting donations to the Boy Scouts because the scouts will not let homosexuals, atheists, and (strangely enough) girls join
MTV, for three reasons: (1) For not letting Rush H. Limbaugh III be a VJ on their music network because he's a conservative; (2) for letting Bill Clinton on their other, and more popular, music network because he's not a conservative; (3) for letting PETA, Greenpeace, and Magic Johnson on their children's network, Nickelodeon, to make sure that children don't become conservatives.

Time-Warner, for distributing Ice-T's CD *Cop Killer*

McDonald's, for its new environmental policy on fast-food containers

Turner Broadcasting, for the disgusting and hypocritical union of monopolistic company owner Ted Turner and known Communist Jane Fonda, and for the conception and birth of their loathsome bastard offspring, *Captain Planet and the Planeteers*

Orion Pictures, for creating *Wayne's World* and the *Bill and Ted* movies. *Any motion picture company that makes movies, TV shows, etc., about two teenagers with their own cable TV show. Or about two teenagers who go joyriding through time, screwing up history, with the help of hippie comedians from the future.*

The New York School System, for doling out condoms to kids

Fox Television, for doling out condoms to kids (on *Beverly Hills, 91202484249457969715465*)

The Christic Institute, for investigating President Bush and his family at the request of Ross Perot. (The Christic Institute has appeared in past E-Lists. This should disprove the myth that Ross Perot is a conservative.)

Planned Parenthood, for out-Hitlering Hitler, out-Staling Stalin, and accepting contributions from Ross Perot

"You asked for groups?" Mr. Siefert continues. "I'll give you groups (rock, that is)":

Nirvana, for putting child pornography on their CD covers

Red Hot Chili Peppers, for trying to put ordinary pornography on their CD covers

Guns N' Roses, for putting vocal pornography in their CDs

Marky Mark and the Funky Bunch, for flag-burning and Bush-bashing

Paxton Helms of Atlanta, Georgia, writes from Europe to condemn:

Any company that takes out a full-page ad in the European Times *to announce that it "[lends] only to companies we believe to be as sound ethically as they are financially."* The ethics, of course, are things like testing cosmetics on dummy rabbits.

And he sends us an example from some hapless Lancaster, England, financial institution called *The Co-operative Bank*, which probably doesn't have anything but moldy carrots to lend anyway.

Rich Hardcastle of Terre Haute, Indiana, rails against:

The Eugene V. Debs Foundation, for giving out awards to further the work of leftist "visionaries" such as Ed Asner, Jesse Jackson, and Peter, Paul and Mary. The foundation is dedicated to keeping socialism on the respirator long enough to revive it when capitalism is discredited.

The Indiana State University Student Government, for funding Native American powwows and other such guilt trips

ISU's Housing Now! chapter, for funding marches against Desert Storm

People for the Ethical Treatment of Animals, for actually calling a student government vice-presidential candidate a "murderer" because he joked about his love of red meat

Patrick Mathias of Manville, New Jersey, takes umbrage at:

Linda Bloodworth-Thomason and Harry Thomason, television producers. The Thomasons are vocal supporters of Bill Clinton [N.B. And produced his sickening "bad stepfather" home movie for the Democratic convention—Ed.] and have his brother on their payroll as a production assistant (*Spy*, July-August 1992). Following the Clarence Thomas hearings, the Thomasons rushed into production an episode of *Designing Women* that may rank as the crudest piece of agitprop since the last PBS documentary about ACT UP. Linda Bloodworth-Thomason subsequently called the *Larry King* show on CNN to denounce the revelations about Clinton's sex life as nothing more than Republican smear tactics. According to former cast member (and, perhaps not coincidentally, Republican) Delta Burke, the Thomasons also sent strongly worded letters to their cast and crew asking for donations to Clinton's campaign.

Another O'Neill, one N. J. of Tracy, California, tells us: "Imagine my surprise when I found this marvelous collection of enemies (with the possible exception of the Pediatric AIDS Foundation) on the back of the latest B-52's CD. I therefore nominate the *B-52's* to serve on the Enemies List for their support of these organizations." The jacket text reads, in part:

STOP! READ BEFORE OPENING
The B-52's support these organizations, which are
among the many working to make the quality
of life better on this planet.
The B-52's encourage you to check out these
worthwhile organizations as well as your local direct action
groups, since we all need to participate to bring about
positive change. We have tried to eliminate the use
of the long box, but where that was not possible,
we have added this useful clip and save.

CLIP AND SAVE
Amnesty International
Common Cause
Greenpeace
National Abortion Rights Action League (NARAL)
National Audubon Society
National Organization for Women (NOW)
Natural Resources Defense Council (NRDC)
The Nature Conservancy
Pediatric AIDS Foundation
People for the American Way
Public Citizen
Rigpe Dorje Foundation
Save the Manatees
Sierra Club

We've spared you the phone numbers of these "organizations," which are listed alongside.

Getting slightly off the eleemosynary track, Irving L. Jacobs of San Diego, California, gleefully roasts:

> *The San Diego Union-Tribune*, ostensibly a conservative daily
> newspaper, for turning over its Arts and Entertainment departments
> to the liberal-left. A red star goes to book editor Arthur Salm, who
> damned *Give War a Chance* for its "fascist sentiments," bashed *The
> Conservative Crack-Up* as the work of a has-been, but who just did
> an adoring, worshipful interview with Molly Ivins, who "gleefully
> roasts right-wingers."

Ronald D. Crockett of Wollaston, Massachusetts, wrote to the United States Office of Personnel Management to complain about the inclusion of the idiotic People for the Ethical Treatment of Animals in the *Combined Federal Campaign*, a United Way–type program that solicits charitable donations in government workplaces. This is from the reply he got:

> In December 1987, Congress passed the first permanent legislation on the
> Combined Federal Campaign (CFC). In that legislation OPM was
> mandated to make the CFC more inclusive rather than exclusive. As a
> result, many new and different types of voluntary agencies have been found
> eligible. . . . Next year's CFC list of eligible charities will probably increase

again. Furthermore, in conformance with the mandate of Congress, it is reasonable to expect that this list will contain groups that some employees may find objectionable. Nevertheless, I expect the past trend to continue and the CFC will have another record year for total contributions.

Sincerely,
Dennis A. Matteotti
CFC Operations

Hope you never need a baboon liver, Dennis.

Marguerite Snow of Stockton, California, admits:

I've lived in California all of my life and I know it's a big state and I know we have more than our share of flakes, but even I was amazed to see how many groups could crawl out from under the woodwork to oppose the liberation of my children from our loathsome teachers' union. And they claim it's only a "partial" list.

She attaches a California Teachers Association/National Education Association advertisement:

On Record Against "Choice/Vouchers"
Groups Agreeing with CTA's Position

American Association of University Women
Americans United for Separation of Church and State
Anti-Defamation League
Black American Political Association of California
California Council of United Auto Workers Retirees
California Democratic Party
California Legislative Council for Older Americans
California National Organization for Women
California State P.T.A.
California State Police Association
Chicano Federation
Coalition of California Welfare Organizations
Coalition of Medical Providers
Committee to Protect the Political Rights of Minorities

*Jewish Community Relations Committee, Jewish Federation Council of
    Greater Los Angeles
Legislative Black Caucus
National Association for the Advancement of Colored People, Region 1
Older Women's League, San Francisco
The Rainbow Coalition
A. Philip Randolph Institute
Raza Administrators and Counselors of Higher Education
Thai Association of Southern California
Unified Vietnamese Community Council*

The above is a partial listing of their partial listing.

Adrian H. Krieg of Woodbridge, Connecticut, forwards a wonderful article from the September 17, 1990, issue of *Forbes*, describing some thirty-five inter-locking and largely tax-free Ralph Nader organizations. Says *Forbes*: "Like all good empire builders, Ralph Nader has created a highly effective organization, the elements of which are tied together by financial and personal relationships." Some of the most egregious Nader metastases, as described by *Forbes*:

> *Center for Auto Safety:* major grants from State Farm and Allstate
>   foundations. Sells litigation kits to lawyers involved in auto
>   litigation
> *Occupational Safety and Health Law Center:* specializing in defending
>   workers' rights and employee suits
> *Center for Science in the Public Interest:* petitions and lobbies for
>   regulation of the food and pesticide industry
> *Citizen Utility Boards:* funding: membership; "intervenor fees" utilities
>   are legally obliged to pay CUB activists
> *Public Citizen, Inc.:* Nader's longtime flagship lobbying litigation group
> *Public Interest Research Groups:* twenty-five state chapters on ninety
>   college campuses. Funding: through mandatory or "negative checkoff"
>   student fees
> *Trial Lawyers for Public Justice Foundation:* activities: class action,
>   precedent-setting suits; litigation clearinghouse
> *Council for Responsible Genetics:* works to restrict recombinant DNA
>   research
> *Institute for Injury Reduction:* funding: plaintiff attorneys. Finances
>   product liability research and media events

107

Consumers Union: co-founded Center for Auto Safety with Nader. Collaborates with Public Citizen to fight against tort reforms.

National Committee for Responsive Philanthropy: lobbies foundations, corporations to give to "progressive" groups

Fund for Constitutional Government: funded in part by General Motors heir Stuart Mott. Its Government Accountability Project works closely with Public Citizen, filing joint amicus briefs against the government.

As if on cue, Matthew G. Mirmak writes from Minneapolis, Minnesota:

> I suggest that you nominate *Augsburg College*, their student senate, and the Naderite chapter of MPIRG (Minnesota Public Interest Research Group) for conspiring to force the student body of Augsburg to pay an additional mandatory fee of $3.75, which is tacked on to our tuition bill, to MPIRG, in order to fund their leftist and downright pinko activities.

Eric T. Fritz of Mauston, Wisconsin, is, like Mr. Mirmak, angry with his midwestern institution of higher learning:

> $47 of my $1,957 student bill at the *University of Wisconsin-Whitewater* goes to the Segregated University Fee Allocation Committee, which in turn goes to groups like the Gay Lesbian Student Union, the Environmental Federation, and RISE, or Resistance to Intervention, Suppression, and Exploitation, a bunch of sixties dropouts and crybabies just to the left of Pol Pot.

Mark Peña of Austin, Texas, sends us the schedule of the University of Texas's "1992 English Department Graduate Colloquium: Pedagogy and Values." Among the various panels offered the lucky participants:

> Feminism, Marxism, and Cultural Activism in the University
> Rethinking Pedagogy in Light of Postmodernism
> Desire in the Classroom: A Pedagogical Rubric
> Coming Out Professionally: The Responsibility of Gay and
>   Straight Faculty
> Gender and Trauma in the Classroom
> Teaching Writing and the Lesbian Subject
> Writing, Power, and Homophobia in the Computer-Mediated Classroom
> Learning Composition and Literature from Women of Color

Teaching Reading and Writing as a History of Competition Between
    Social Discourses
The Cultural Trope of Literacy and the Rhetoric of Grammar
The Shifting Subject(s) of Literary Study; or, How Do You Spell
    'Hegemony'?

We need hardly say that Mr. Peña would like the *U.T. English Department*
added to the Enemies List.

J. Lloyd Simms of Barnegat, New Jersey, detests:
Warner Bros., for funding Spike Lee's Malcolm X movie when they
    could've used that money toward *Batman 3*
Network executives, for giving millions of dollars' worth of free publicity
    to Sister Souljah by booking her on such shows as *Larry King*,
    Today, etc., etc.

Robert P. Fairchild of Arlington, Virginia, gives a Bronx cheer to:
Michael Wood, PBS personality and putative archaeologist, described as
    "writer and presenter" of *Legacy*, whose final installment ("The
    Barbarian West") concludes with one-world platitudes and ravings in
    the genre of apocalyptic environmentalism
And points out that *Maryland Public Television*, *NHK* (Enterprises?), *MFS*
(Mutual Fund Services?), and the *Corporation for Public Broadcasting* were all
listed in the credits as sources of funding for *Legacy*.

Dr. Tom Bohr of Redlands, California, would have us spin the dial on:
KPFK, a Los Angeles–area station located somewhere near Tom
    Hayden's haunt of Berkeley-South, Santa Monica. It is part of the
    "Radio Pacifica" (Pacifistica?) network. Besides promoting the rantings
    of nuclear winter nutcake and pseudo scientist Helen Caldicott, they
    were proud to offer airtime to Louis Farrakhan henchman Steve Cokely
    of Chicago. Cokely insinuated that federal officials set some of the
    L.A. riot fires. He is better known for accusing Jewish doctors of
    injecting blacks with AIDS.

Paul Pakala of Appleton, Wisconsin, vents his spleen upon the *New York
State Arts Council*: "I feel they deserve an evening in a burned-out theater, sitting in urine, listening to lesbian rap singers, and wearing tie-dyed T-shirts."

John Doughty of Monrovia, California, mails us the *National Chicano
Moratorium Committee*'s "wanted" poster of Christopher Columbus. The great

misplacer of India is accused of "grand theft, genocide, racism, initiating the destruction of a culture, rape, torture and maiming of indigenous people."

Scott Forrest of Brooklyn Park, Minnesota, is a consumer-activist consumer of *Consumer Reports*. He suggests they be recalled for "their constant sermonizing about the homeless, the 'environment,' and socialized medicine. I wish they would spare me the lectures and just tell me which VCR to buy."

Eric J. Paddon of Devon, Pennsylvania, avers:

My nominee for the Enemies List is *Comedy Central*, an irritating cable TV channel which on the average serves up two hours of decent programming (Jack Benny, Steve Allen) and twenty-two hours of pinko propaganda. [Eric, are you *sure* about Steve?—Ed.] In addition to the usual group of talentless stand-up comics who think they can get a laugh by uttering the name "Ronald Reagan" in a sarcastic manner, the worst abuser is a series known as *Mystery Science Theater 3000*.

The premise of the series isn't too bad. A naive geek and his two robots are stranded in space and forced to watch bad movies that they talk back to. However, their forays into political satire always end up on the pink side.

Case in point: While talking back to a bad science fiction movie in which aliens brainwash earthlings to do their bidding, the stupefied human begins to walk about in a daze and offers up this bit of sarcasm: "Now I understand, Ronald Reagan was a great president."

Kevin J. Hritz—what is it with the middle initial "J." among us incredibly talented and sensitive people?—of St. Mary's, Pennsylvania, proscribes:
General Electric, for those saccharine multicultural ads on *This Week with David Brinkley*
One World Ted's little outfit in Atlanta, [*CNN*, for the] disgusting *The People Bomb* series shown during May of 1992. I hope he takes the advice of the series and decides to forgo the creation of his progeny with Miss Hanoi 1972
Pennsylvania State University, for creating the Office of the Vice Provost of Underrepresented Groups
Any group or corporation that actually pays to sponsor a $10,000 Anita Hill speech. You know who you are.
The Institute of Electrical and Electronic Engineers. I never thought it would happen, but in the latest issue of its house publication *Spectrum*, the cover story, "Diversity in the Engineering

Workplace," discusses sexual orientation. I suppose I will now have to show that my designs contain 10 percent gay/lesbian/bisexual engineering content before I can land accounts with really big corporations.

The Reverend James H. Fladland of Richmond, Virginia, is a professional in the field of sin and knows an enemy of God and man when he sees one:

> Much as it pains me to do so, I must nominate the denomination of which I am an ordained clergyman for this year's Enemies List. *The Evangelical Lutheran Church in America* has proved itself to be the most PC church body in the U.S., not just for the usual stuff (e.g., Columbus-bashing and *New Masses*–sounding "socioeconomic analyses") but by ensconcing in its very constitution the hideous principle of racial, sexual, and linguistic quotas.

Timothy C. Reiner of Worchester, Massachusetts, will rent some John Wayne videos and eschew:
> *WGBH* (Channel 2) and *WGBX* (Channel 44), for hectoring the good people of eastern Massachusetts with left-wing PBS propaganda, much of it at their own expense, and for scheduling Bill Buckley's *Firing Line* at eleven o'clock on Sunday nights

Dr. Edward B. Elmer of Pleasanton, Texas, decries:
> *The Nature Conservancy* ("Fifth Amendment—what Fifth Amendment?")
> *CBS "News"* (lovers of Leonard "I Wuz Framed" Peltier)
> *Any and all teachers' unions*
> *The AMA* (the newest gun control lobby)
> *The Boston Globe*
> *The Boston Globe*
> *The Boston Globe*

Carl L. Rowley, Jeffrey E. Asbed, and Jon M. Moyers of St. Louis, Missouri, being lawyers all, bring a bill of attainder against:
> *The Peace Corps*, because its name contains the word "peace," and because it arrogantly and mistakenly implies that the corps' "mission" could conceivably prevent war, or even an argument between pygmies over who cooks the cat tonight. (And for doing so with money that was not its until it took it from us.)
> *The National Education Association*, because its non-merit-based-pay, six-hour-per-day, nine-month-per-year members refuse to take competency examinations, purportedly for reasons other than their own incompetence. And because most of them are Communists.

Sean Smith of Weehawken, New Jersey, goes right to the top when he's mad. He has it in for:

> *Matthew*, who misquoted Jesus in 19:23. The actual quote was "It is *easier* for a rich man to enter the gates of Heaven than for a camel to pass through the eye of a needle," not the other way around. If Old Matty hadn't screwed that up we wouldn't have Liberation Theology, Vatican II, or the Christic Institute.

Neither rain nor snow nor Victoria's Secret catalogs stop mailman Art Vasterling once he gets going:

> I want to see all nonprofit mailing discontinued with the exception of material for the blind. I know this makes me a heretic in both the union and the post office by insisting that we rid ourselves of every person and/or function that does not move mail. But our body politic is riddled with those who use the U.S. Mail for fund-raising to attack my lifestyle and culture. The latest lousebag lobby is the *Native American Rights Fund*, which appeared last fall. They are soliciting donations for protest and bail bonds to be utilized in the spoilage and ruination of every Columbian Celebration within their reach.

Art, by the way, did not provide us with a return address.

J. J. Rose of Boston, Massachusetts, says:

> The Brother Can You Spare a Billion medal is pinned to the derrière of the *stockholders of American car companies*. These patsies dole out tens of millions in salaries and perks to their executives, who then become globetrotting mendicants asking for protection against Japan. There was a time when the "protection" against foreign competition was a good product, not congressional action. But, hey, why do it the hard way if Uncle Sap will foot the bill?

Joe A-something, whose last name is illegible but who identifies himself as "the only sagebrush Republican male nurse in America," has put down the bedpan and picked up the gun:

Stand back! I don't want you to get hit with any shrapnel:

The African National Congress
The World Wildlife Fund
The National Conference of Mayors
The ACLU (Too obvious, huh?)
The Albuquerque Chapter of the NAACP (for the Bobby Knight flap)

The Staff at the Oregonian (a nest of pathological liars posing as a newspaper)
Lawrence Walsh's gang of thugs
The Oregon Peace Institute (What does their "I believe you, Anita"
    bumper sticker have to do with world peace?)
People for the American Way
Time *magazine* (Watch out, *U.S. News & World Report.* You're heading
    down the same path.)
Physicians for Social Responsibility (a bunch of bell-bottomed finger-
    pointers who feel guilty about their adjusted gross incomes)
The World Health Organization (for inviting Liz Taylor to lecture on
    matters of personal hygiene)
The National Commission on AIDS (for promulgating the biggest fraud
    since "Camelot")
And, finally *(Pull! . . . Kaboom!)*, the *Republican Party* (for piddling
    away the greatest intellectual revolution since $E = MC^2$).

Todd Davis of Kentwood, Michigan, excommunicates:
All the churches whose leaders apparently live by this revised version of
the Ten Commandments:
   I.   You shall have no other gods before the Federal Government of the
      United States.
   II.   You shall not make for yourself an idol in the form of anything on
      the earth, but worship the earth itself.
   III.   Do not take Jesse Jackson's name in vain.
   IV.   Remember the anniversary of *Roe* v. *Wade* and keep it holy.
   V.   Honor your mother, your mother's boyfriend, your father's boyfriend, etc.
   VI.   You may not kill criminals who have been convicted of heinous
      crimes, but feel free to kill human fetuses of all ages.
   VII.   You may not commit adultery—without a condom.
   VIII.   You may not steal—except from the rich or during a riot.
   IX.   You may not give false testimony—except when attempting to keep
      Clarence Thomas off the Supreme Court.
   X.   You shall not covet anything that belongs to your neighbor—except
      for the purpose of redistributing the wealth.

Jennifer L. Durham of (and this must cause some confusion for Mr. Vasterling
and his fellow post officers) Raleigh, North Carolina, inveighs against "the assort-
ment of ridiculous government agencies easily found in any phone book. Here's
a sampling from the Raleigh listings":
    The Disabilities Governor's Advocacy Council
    Youth Advocacy and Involvement Office

The Adult Health Division's Divisions of Refugee Health and Migrant Health
The Plant Industry Division's Bee Program
The Inmate Grievance Commission
The Division of Environmental Health's Shellfish Sanitation Branch
The Facility Services Division of Bingo Licensing
Felony Diversion Program (Is this a new euphemism for prison?)
Parent to Parent (?)
The Labor Department's Health and Safety Department's Elevator and Amusement Device Division (Whew!)
The Barber Examiners Licensing Board
North Carolina Center for International Understanding

And she adds "the following stupid items and regulations funded and/or enforced with taxpayer money":

Abnormally low speed limits (which includes most of them)
A new law in North Carolina (and probably other places) requiring motorists to turn on their headlights if it's raining hard enough to use the windshield wipers
A new regulation in some states prohibiting one to return to a salad bar with a dirty plate

Robert L. Hamilton of Edmonton, Alberta, can't help himself:

I know this list is only supposed to contain institutions, associations, etc., but I can't help myself. I have to nominate the *boneheads in our Province of Ontario* for electing a socialist government just when the rest of the world is turning the silly buggers out of their legislatures. (P.S. If you must have an institution, I nominate the *Canadian Broadcasting Corporation*.)

Vincent Frattaruolo of Palm Beach, Florida, whose critical sense is a lot sharper than his handwriting, scribbles a reproof of:

The International Commission on English in the Liturgy, the organization responsible for the introduction of gender-neutral language in the Catholic Mass

Matt Stuart of Altoona, Iowa, rebukes:

The Creators of TV's Star Trek—The Next Generation, *for trying to make the future politically correct*

Lawrence D. Skutch of Westport, Connecticut, spotted this howler:

> *Trustees of the John F. Kennedy Library Foundation*, who gave this
> year's Profiles in Courage award to Lowell Weicker because he
> raised taxes rather than taking the more difficult and courageous
> route by cutting spending

Dr. Dennis J. (there it is again) Doolin of Tokyo, Japan, doesn't have any
nominations to the Enemies List. Perhaps still reeling after President Bush's
visit, he writes to ask a simple question: "I've been in Tokyo for the past fifteen
years. Is some diabolical group lacing our nation's reservoirs with mind-altering
substances?"

The short answer, Dr. Doolin, is yes.

And, on this year's E-List, we give the last word to Warren Wetmore of
Hazel Crest, Illinois:

> Who subventions the Sinistrals? We could round up the usual suspects—
> the Ford Foundation, the MacArthur Foundation, the Rockefeller
> Foundation (whose conservative founders continue to redline their
> tachometers, spinning in their graves). Fools contributing to knaves is
> strictly dog-bites-man. However, if we really want to de-fund the left, we
> must hold an emergency competency hearing on the biggest spastic,
> drooling, brain-dead Daddy Dumbbucks of them all: *THE
> GOVERNMENT OF THE UNITED STATES OF AMERICA.*

(Editors' Note: We are very disappointed that no one mentioned Benetton. *We
don't know how much money this corporation gives to Commies, but it certainly
gives a lot of bad ideas to kids in shopping malls: "Hey, Muffy, look, a picture
of starving people! Way cool! Makes me totally want to buy a sweater!")*

THE
PETER UEBERROTH GOLD MEDAL FOR
100-METER-DASH-
CARRYING-A-VCR

Now for the second part of our mission, wherein laurels are awarded to public figures who praised, encouraged, downplayed, excused, or called for
"understanding of" the L.A. riots:

Helen H. Bergman of New York, New York, sends us a copy of the June 12, 1992, *Public Employee Press*, the newspaper of New York's District Council 37 of the AFL-CIO American Federation of State, County, and Municipal Employees (there's nothing like the U.S. labor movement for windy monikers, now that the Kremlin is gone). In this august publication, *Stanley Hill*, executive director of District Council 37, is quoted addressing the annual convention of the Coalition of Black Trade Unionists: "'CBTU's theme—bringing our communities together—was made even more relevant by the damage caused by dreams deferred,' Hill said, when delegates toured L.A., seeing the devastation first-hand."

Steven Carter, who lives in L.A. and was "seeing the devastation first-hand" big time, mails us a brochure from the *Liberty Hill Foundation*. What they mean by "Hill" is probably Beverly, possibly Anita. What they mean by "Liberty" we shudder to think:

> The Liberty Hill Foundation announces the "Fund for a New L.A." to assist organizations working for racial equality, democratic planning, and community economic development in the aftermath of the Rodney King verdict and Los Angeles uprising. . . . Through a generous donation from Comic Relief, the Liberty Hill Foundation has created a special fund to help community organizations respond to the challenges posed by the recent riots in Los Angeles.
> The goal of the "Fund for a New L.A." is to enable community organizations to promote institutional change to solve the injustices which helped to create the Los Angeles upheaval: poverty, racial tensions, police brutality, and urban violence.

Edward Flynn of Garland, Texas, states:

> My nominees for the "Uebie," whose primary distinguishing features seemed to be opening every monologue with "there is no excuse for this kind of behavior" and then going on for ten minutes excusing it, are *Maxine Waters* and *Bryant Gumbel*.

John C. Morrison of Windsor, Connecticut, makes three awards:
> *Boy Clinton*, as quoted in the *New York Times* on May 2: "To them, it sort of stands for all the neglect, all the economic decline, all the

insecurity in the streets, and not being able to walk safely on the
streets." Well now, what better way to make the streets safe? If one
is afraid to stroll, start a riot!
  A walking miracle named *Lourdes Baird*, U.S. attorney in L.A.,
said there was no racial element in the beating near to death
delivered to Mr. Reginald Denny. This gem was quoted
straight-faced in the *New York Times* on May 14. She is
pursuing racial bias charges against the police in the King case.
  The *New York Times*, for absolute and total unmitigated nonsense
in every word they saw fit to print

And Mr. Morrison further notes that no one "will admit that 'Checkday,' May
2, had the most to do with stopping the riots, when the post office refused to
deliver. People had to line up for blocks to get their checks!"

  Robert Kord of Cutler, Maine, proposes a shared medal in a "bulsh conglom-
erate category":
  Paul Wellstone
  Jane Fonda and mouth-mate
  Patricia Schroeder
  M. Gorbachev
  Patti Davis

  Ed Busca of Chicago, Illinois, hands the palm to L.A. mayor *Tom Bradley*
for inflammatory remarks after the King trial decision and notes that "if
Hizzoner Mayor Daley I or II had said anything resembling Honorable Tom's
blast, he would have been burned at the stake."

  Rich Hardcastle of Terre Haute, Indiana, who has already done some fine
work on our Enemies List above, returns to confer honors upon:
  kristina marie korobov, who, as the first female Student Government
    president at Indiana State University, not only forgot how to capitalize
    her name but also called a public forum of "understanding," which
    resulted in near fistfights and similar versions of harmony in the wake of
    the L.A. riots

  Dan Buksa of Munster, Indiana, yearns to suitably reward:
  Sister Souljah, who "raps" that "blacks should take a week off from work
    to kill whites"

Roy O'Grady of Goose Creek, South Carolina, gives the prize to
    Arsenio Hall: He was useless in stopping the riots once they had started,
        and he gave the gang members of L.A. a forum for their beliefs without
        ever questioning the sincerity of these drug-dealing, murderous thugs.

Barbara Morgan of Hot Springs, Arkansas, tells us: "During the CNN coverage, I was amazed to see a tall, nattily dressed black man identified only as the *'Mayor of Compton'* invite the local Koreans to 'leave town.' This was replayed numerous times, but nary a word against this type of racial invective was heard from *any* commentator."

John P. Doremus of Tallahassee, Florida, proposes Gold, Silver, Bronze, Cement, and Mud medals to:
    Donahue/*ABC*
    Donahue's guest Al Sharpton
    Maxine Waters (please!)
    Mayor Tom Bradley
    The Today Show/*NBC*
As Mr. Doremus explains, "All of the above loudly condemned in a public forum the King verdict hours after it was announced and thus aided, furthered, and encouraged the riots that followed."

Jeffrey D. Van Schaick, of parts unknown, alerts us to a scathing criticism of the *Los Angeles Times*'s riot coverage that appeared in the *Wall Street Journal*. The article, written by Scott Shuger, states: "In the face of all that video and the *Times*'s own extensive accounts of unprovoked assaults and widespread looting and arson, the paper did what it could do to fuzz up the issue of personal responsibility for those actions." And goes on to prove it. Mr. Van Schaick says: "On behalf of Mr. Shuger, I nominate the *Los Angeles Times*."

Stephanie Gutmann of New York, New York, believes another garland should go to the *Los Angeles Times*'s East Coast evil twin: "OK, a newspaper isn't an individual or a public figure, but don't you think the *New York Times*'s editorial board deserves the Peter Ueberroth Gold Medal for declaring, in its lead editorial, on May 3, while the rubble in L.A. was still smouldering, that 'America consigns great numbers of young black men to lawless lives'?"

Patrick Mathias, who also contributed to this year's E-List, returns to present a couple of blue ribbons (tied in a noose) to:

Luke Perry, "star of *Beverly Hills, 90210*," quoted in the July *Vanity Fair*: "It's symbolic; we're living in a society that's getting out of control. I don't think it's a race issue. . . . I saw white people down there screaming last night. I saw Hispanics. I saw Asians. I saw blacks. There were gays. There were straights. If nothing else, I see some beauty in what's happening. You've got people you would ordinarily never see together . . . "

Ronald Walters, chairman of the political science department of Howard University, in a bylined article that appeared in a number of newspapers, including the June 23 *News Tribune* in Woodbridge, New Jersey: "The depth and power of Sister Souljah's art may make some people anxious, but her voice represents an authentic expression of sentiment among a substantial segment of black youth and black people. . . . Sister Souljah . . . has gone beyond merely rapping to use her considerable intelligence as a community organizer for productive causes in the black community . . . "

We really can't give this medal too often to *Maxine Waters*. As James Gidwitz of Chicago, Illinois, puts it:

My nominee for the "Peter Ueberroth Medal" removes the notion of contest from this award. That is, of course, the *Honorable* (Hello?) *Maxine Waters*, local congressperson. While her unfortunate presence on the television coverage initially added a welcome counterpoint of comedy to the mayhem and looting, she quickly became a nauseating apologist for criminal behavior and demanded that new federal subsidies be created to somehow reward it. This must have been a blow to her many law-abiding constituents—especially those of Korean descent, whom she unilaterally disenfranchised.

Buzz Brockway of Lawrenceville, Georgia, slings a wreath at:
Clark-Atlanta University, whose students felt such compassion for
        Rodney King that they looted Macy's and lots of liquor stores
And Mr. Brockway bids farewell to police chief *Daryl Gates*, who is handed a Uebie "for being a spineless wonder and allowing the riots to simmer unchecked for days."

Lastly, Steven Segers of Victorville, California, would present our coveted prize to the whole and entire city of "Lost" Angeles:

From the first images of watching the police run from dangerous criminals because they weren't allowed to use the necessary force to control the situation, to the subsequent scenes of police treating looters with a how-may-I-help-you-service-with-a-smile mentality, Los Angeles is a typical example of liberalism run amok: soft on crime, hard on the police, and blame it all on Ronald Reagan.

MISCELLANEOUS NEW ENEMIES LIST
HOUSEKEEPING ITEMS

We take this opportunity to give our special thanks to the following "Friends of the Enemies List":

To Henry Beard and Chris Cerf, for their hilarious (and painstakingly documented) compendium, *The Official Politically Correct Dictionary and Handbook*, the footnotes to which are a whole New Enemies List in themselves. *TOPCDH* is available in a handsome paperback edition from Villard Books, a division of Random House, and is priced so as to be affordable to the oppressed. Read it and weep tears of simultaneous laughter and rage in a nonheretical modality of deconstructivist postmodernism.

To the NRA, which published an excellent article about the L.A. riots in the July issues of both its *American Hunter* and *American Rifleman* magazines. The eye- (and peep sight–) witness account was written by James Jay Baker and appropriately titled, "Second Amendment Message in Los Angeles." As we NRA members like to say, "Join or die."

To Betty Friedan, for putting the McCarthy Era ur-Enemies List into perspective. She was interviewed by *People* magazine at a party celebrating the new HBO movie *Citizen Cohn*, which is about Tail-Gunner Joe's old pal Roy Cohn. Betty says the movie "will teach a whole generation about one of the most evil men who ever lived." Stand aside, Hitler and Pol Pot.

And extra special thanks to Woody Allen—just in case there was anybody out there who still believed in psychoanalysis or thought East Coast intellectuals weren't living piles of slime.

Well, so long for now. We'll leave you with this edifying tale from the October 11, 1991, *Boston Herald*:

The night of May 13, 1984, David Freeman, a Duxbury firefighter, crept into the room where his wife was sleeping and beat her so severely with a club that her injuries are lifelong.

Concern over Freeman's mental stability prompted the Board of Selectmen to remove him from his job.

Last month, the Massachusetts Commission Against Discrimination—noting Freeman was found innocent of assault by reason of temporary insanity—cited the town for "handicap discrimination."

The MCAD restored the fifty-two-year-old Freeman to his job and awarded him $200,000 for back pay and emotional distress plus 12 percent interest. ❖

⟪ VII ⟫

Enemies in the White House

The American Spectator, November 1993

This list has been limited to members and cohorts of the Clinton administration, those simps and ninnies, lava-lamp liberals and condo pinks, spoiled twerps, wiffenpoofs, ratchet-jawed purveyors of monkey doodle and baked wind, piddlers upon merit, beggars at the door of accomplishment, thieves of livelihood, envy-coddling tax lice applauding themselves for their magnanimity with the money of others, their nose in virtue's bum. They are the Lhasa apsos of Poli Sci returning to the vomit of liberalism, little boar pigs looking to rut with that sow-who-eats-her-young, the welfare state, squamous muck-dwellers bottom-feeding on the worries and disappointments of the electorate—ditch carp of democracy.

When have we seen such an administration of pukes and feebs? The president and his spawn, incubi at the public teat, surpass Kennedy in their arrogance, Johnson in their lack of scruples, and Carter in their plain stupidity. They are dung beetles in legislation, legislators in the bed chamber, chambermaids on the battlefield, and field marshals in the war against everything reasonable and decent. Suchlike has not passed through that large intestine which is the Executive Branch since Franklin Delano Roosevelt was wheeled up the disabled access ramp to the gates of Hell.

But wait. I could be wrong. Possibly I've failed to learn anything from all the marvelous work that's been done by social scientists over the past three-quarters of a century. Perhaps Clinton and his appointees aren't evil. Perhaps they're sick. And maybe what we think is disorganization, incompetence, mendacity, folly, pandering, and Marxism-sold-by-the-drink is actually a plea for help. If this is true and the Clinton administration is a form of mass psychosis, there's only one thing to do. We must return these people to private life as quickly as possible, by impeachment if necessary. Once the Clintonites are ordinary citizens again, they will be able to receive the mental health care of which they are in such dire need—and all for free, thanks to national health care reforms spearheaded by the First Lady.

It's likely that the president himself is crazy, at least if the *Psychiatric Dictionary* published by Bill's alma mater Oxford University is anything to go by:

> *lying, pathological.* Falsification entirely disproportionate to any
> discernible end in view; such lying rarely, if ever, centers about a single
> event; usually it manifests itself over a period of years, or even a lifetime.

Of course, the *vice* president is a loon, too. And an incoherent one. Below is a verbatim transcript from the June 3, 1993, ABC *Nightline* show where Gore attempted to defend Clinton's withdrawal of the Lani Guinier nomination. Ted Koppel has just asked Gore, "Can you . . . tell me what it is they disagreed on?"

Vice Pres. Gore: The theories—the ideas she expressed about equality of results within legislative bodies and with—by outcome, by decisions made by legislative bodies, ideas related to proportional voting as a general remedy, not in particular cases where the circumstances make that a feasible idea. . . .

Or, if you think the V.P. just had had a little too much Miracle-Gro that day, try reading his book, *Earth in the Balance*:

The cleavage in the modern world between mind and body, man and nature, has created a new kind of addiction: I believe that our civilization is, in effect, addicted to the consumption of the earth itself.

   . . . A person who is not "grounded" in body as well as mind, in feelings as well as thoughts, can pose a threat to whatever he or she touches. We tend to think of the powerful currents of creative energy circulating through every one of us as benign, but they can be volatile and dangerous if not properly grounded.

Those are from a random glance at pages 220–21 in the tree-wasting, error-clogged paperback edition of *EITB*.

So Bill and Al are nutty. This brings us to Vince Foster. Foster has no place on the Enemies List. There was no disgrace in what he did. (No one dies of disgrace in Washington; the whole town would be Ur.) And we don't want to heap abuse on someone who has so recently become a Good Democrat.

But there are no exemptions for those who are deranged and wacky and *bad*. There's Jeffrey Dahmer to be considered—and Ellen Goodman. We didn't declare a truce in World War II just because Hitler needed lithium. We didn't unilaterally disarm just because Stalin was running with one wheel in the sand.

As Vince Foster said, "Here ruining people is considered sport." Play ball!

Maya Angelou
Thirty-two years ago, dead, white, European male Robert Frost wrote a poem for a presidential inauguration. It went, in part, like this:

Some poor fool has been saying in his heart
Glory is out of date in life and art.
Our venture in revolution and outlawry
Has justified itself in freedom's story
Right down to now in glory upon glory.

Hark now to Angelou's "On the Pulse of Morning":

> *Your armed struggles for profit*
> *Have left collars of waste upon*
> *My shore, currents of debris upon my breast.*
> *Yet today I call you to my riverside,*
> *If you will study war no more.*

Such is progress in the Clinton years.

Tipper Gore

The September-October 1993 issue of the new magazine for yuppie breeders, *Family Life*, quotes Mrs. Gore:

> "We were coming home from lunch with their dad, and the kids pointed out a homeless woman on the street," says Tipper. "They wanted to take her home. I explained we couldn't do that, but that each of us could do something." She went on to cofound Families for the Homeless, a nonpartisan partnership of congressional, administration and media families to raise public awareness about homeless people and their needs.

And there you have the morality of liberalism in a nutshell. Help people? No. Give them a buck? Of course not. What the true sanctimonious liberal does is "raise public awareness." This is the U.N.-in-Sarajevo school of good works. Tipper, America's bag ladies thank you from the bottom of their, um, paper bags.

The various scads and oodles of children sired by Al ("No goal is more crucial to healing the global environment than stabilizing human population." —*EITB*, p. 307) Gore are not on this Enemies List, however. The same article in *Family Life* has Tipper telling us: "The Halloween the kids like to recount best is when Al dressed up as a carrot."

Sharp as tacks, those Gore kids—they noticed.

Ron Brown

Clinton's secretary of commerce is suspected of having engaged in—you guessed it—commerce. The FBI is investigating allegations that Brown received $700,000 from the Vietnamese government in return for promoting free trade. We don't want any of that—NAFTA or no NAFTA, this is a Democratic administration. Not to worry, Ron, even if the accusations are true, by the time you get done paying Clinton-era income taxes, that bribery offense will be only misdemeanor-sized.

Secretary of State Warren Christopher,
U.N. Ambassador Madeleine Albright, and
National Security Adviser Anthony Lake
According to the August 19, 1993, edition of America's *Izvestia*, the *Boston Globe*, these three lukewarm warriors are urging the president to allow U.S. combat troops to regularly serve in United Nations peacekeeping missions under the command of U.N. officers. So, when your boy is ordered into battle backward, armed only with a sharp stick, by Eleventy-Star General Mumbungle Butthole of the Republic of Bulemia, you'll know where to address your letters of complaint.

Warren Christopher
Again, I refer those with short memories to Daniel Wattenberg's article "Clinton's Hard-Line Appeaser" in the February 1993 issue of the *American Spectator*. Here Mr. Wattenberg described how Delta Force commander Colonel Charlie Beckwith briefed President Carter and the nation's top security advisers on the plan to rescue American hostages being held by Iranian Revolutionary Guards. "Anyone who is holding a hostage," said Beckwith, "we intend to shoot him right between the eyes."

According to Beckwith, who is one of our country's most highly decorated soldiers, Christopher's reply was, "Well, would you consider shooting them in the leg, or in the ankle or the shoulder?"

Janet Reno
Addressing the National Black Prosecutors Association, the attorney general said, "We have to do something about guns. If only this nation would rise up and tell the NRA to get lost!" Wait a minute, Stretch, "rise up," or at least maintaining the option to do so, is why we've *got* those guns. Maybe next time you should try making that speech to the survivors of the Warsaw ghetto, or folks who were in Hungary in 1956 or Czechoslovakia in 1968 or Bosnia right now.

P.S. We didn't notice any NRA officials shooting people in Waco.

A Whole Bunch of Future Ex-Senators and Soon-to-Be Former Congressmen
We know the Democrats love the poor because they just created so many more of them. Landslide Billy's tax package passed the Senate 51 to 50 and the House 218 to 216. This makes every pol who said "aye" personally responsible for the economic rape of the nation. In Washington it's being called "The Vince Foster Vote."

Bruce Babbitt
We remember the interior secretary from his 1988 presidential primary campaign. He's not protecting plant life, he *is* plant life.

Marian Wright Edelman

Head of the Children's Defense Fund and the Fagin of family law. Note how the left has quit trying to be a vanguard to anybody large or healthy enough to punch them in the nose; modern Bolshies pester the crippled, the diseased, and, of course, kids. But kids grow up. And they remember. Take our advice, Marian, and stick to Animal Rights or House Plant Liberation or campaigning for Al Gore.

George Stephanopoulos

Beneath contempt in every sense of the phrase—besides, why bother to attack someone when his haircut is doing it for you? Apparently the President of the United States gets some licks in, too. According to Fred Barnes in the September 6, 1993, issue of the *New Republic*, George's principal role in the West Wing is "lightning rod for Clinton's temper tantrums." Mr. Barnes quotes a senior White House official as saying, "Every president has a lot of frustration. They have a need to blow occasionally. George is someone the president can do that to." We certainly hope mere verbal abuse is being discussed here and that the senior White House official was making no innuendos.

Donna Shalala

The January 23, 1993, issue of *Human Events* reprinted long excerpts from a speech the secretary of health and human services delivered at the University of Chicago on November 15, 1991.

Shalala used the speech to describe an ideal world of the future, as seen through the eyes of "Renata," a typical four-year-old kindergarten student in 2004:

> Renata doesn't know any moms who don't work, but she knows lots of moms who are single. She knows some children who only live with their dads, and children who have two dads. . . .
>
> [After her kindergarten class is over Renata goes to a small day-care center operated by a] neighbor who takes care of five children in her home. The backyard of the home is a playground which has been constructed with grant money from the city.
>
> Sometimes [Renata] and her best friend, Josh, play trucks; sometimes they play mommy and daddy, and Josh always puts the baby to bed and changes the diapers, just like his own dad does at home.
>
> At Thanksgiving time, Renata's teacher will tell a story about how people from Europe came to the United States, where the Indians lived. She will say, "It was just the same as if someone had come into your yard and taken all your toys and told you they weren't yours anymore."

Shalala finished her speech by saying that these things would come to pass because "we made it our top priority in our communities and in our Congress."

When Shalala was chancellor of the University of Wisconsin, she championed a ban on language that would be "demeaning" to any "race, sex, religion, color, creed, disability, sexual orientation, national ancestry or age." We say, "Hey, Donna, you ofay broad, you crap-worshiping putty-faced Stalinist retard, molester of dogs and honorary citizen of North Korea, you're old."

Admiral William J. Crowe

The former chairman of the Joint Chiefs of Staff and the next ambassador to the Court of St. James was the only military man above the rank of idiot to support Bill Clinton. Crowe's previous bright idea was to use economic sanctions to get Saddam Hussein out of Kuwait. That is, we were supposed to put a money squeeze on somebody who was sitting on top of a third of the world's oil. In your next lifetime, Matey, a commission awaits you in the navy of Chad.

Harry Thomason and Linda Bloodworth-Thomason

"If Mark Twain were alive today, he would be writing in television," said Linda in an interview in the *New York Times*.

"It may be called the Master Passion, the hunger for self-approval," said Mark Twain in *What Is Man?*

Robert E. Rubin

That layer of hypocritical slime which coats all liberalism has never been thicker than it is upon this former head of the Goldman Sachs investment house. Ex–bucket shop operator Bob made $29.3 million in 1992, taxed at nice, low Republican rates. Now that he's got his pile, he's over at the OEOB stealing money from old people and middle-class professionals. Nor is this his only foray into white-collar crime. Rubin sent a letter from the White House to his former investment banking clients saying, "I also look forward to continuing to work with you in my new capacity." There's a place in the federal system for Robert E. Rubin—the place just vacated by Michael Milken.

Mickey Kantor

While we're on the subject of moral ooze and goo, let us not forget the United States trade representative. We are going to make a rare exception in Mickey's case and quote a *New York Times* editorial someplace other than in the "Current Wisdom" section of the *American Spectator*. The following appeared on May 27, 1993:

Mickey Kantor ... is a busy man. He's in charge of the nation's effort to reduce foreign trade barriers and increase opportunities for American businesses to expand abroad. He sees nothing wrong with helping the Democratic Party in his off hours to raise money by providing private briefings in his office for big-ticket contributors.

At the very least, the public is owed an accounting of who gets to walk the red carpet.

Strobe Talbott

As comsymps go, the ambassador-at-large to the former Soviet republics gets points for persistence. Even after the Coms went, he kept on symping. In an extraordinarily fatuous piece titled "Rethinking the Red Menace" in the January 1, 1990 issue of *Time*, Talbott opined:

> It is a solipsistic delusion to think the West could bring about the seismic events now seizing the USSR and its "fraternal" neighbors. If the Soviet Union had ever been as strong as the threatmongers believed, it would not be undergoing its current upheavals. Those events are actually a repudiation of the hawkish conventional wisdom that has largely prevailed over the past 40 years.

Morton Halperin

Talbott is a mere useful idiot and fellow traveler. Halperin is an actual traitor to his nation. Instead of hanging him, however, the Clinton administration has nominated him to a newly created position in the Defense Department—the (get this for an Orwellian title) assistant secretary of defense for democracy and peacekeeping. The *Washington Times*, in an editorial on June 28, 1993, described Halperin thus:

> He is a former Nixon administration official who had his phone tapped by the FBI because he was suspected of leaking information to the press about the secret U.S. bombing of Cambodia in 1969. He is a former American Civil Liberties Union lawyer who defended the right of the ultraradical *Progressive* magazine in 1979 to publish a recipe for the hydrogen bomb; who aided and abetted ex–CIA agent Philip Agee in his campaign during the 70's to expose the identities of CIA agents overseas, which is believed to have resulted in the murder of the CIA's Athens station chief; who unabashedly avowed, in print and in congressional testimony, his opposition to any and all covert intelligence operations; who, just before the Persian Gulf war, urged

federal employees to come forward with any information indicating the Bush administration was withholding the full truth about its actions in the Gulf. He is a former member of the Carnegie Endowment for International Peace who believes the United States should never intervene militarily anywhere without an invitation from the United Nations.

Joycelyn Elders

You've got to love a Surgeon General who's in such serious need of a StairMaster. If she can hand out condoms in the schools, why can't we hand out pistols? The guns would be strictly for protection against threats to the students' health—such as getting shot first. And the kids would be told that abstaining from killing people is always a valid option.

Bernard Nussbaum

The White House counsel advised Clinton to fight for Zoë Baird's nomination despite her illegal nanny troubles; interviewed Kimba Wood but failed to discover that she had nanny problems, too; countenanced White House staff pressure on the FBI during Travelgate; gave a thumbs-up to Lani Guinier; and waited almost thirty hours before giving Vince Foster's suicide note to the authorities. Actually, strike Bernie off our list—he's obviously an RNC plant.

Roberta Achtenberg

The Clinton-appointee Bad Taste Award goes to the assistant secretary for fair housing at the Department of Housing and Urban Development. In San Francisco's 1992 Gay Pride Parade, Roberta rode in a white convertible, kissing and embracing her girlfriend, San Francisco Municipal Court Judge Mary Morgan, while Judge Morgan's seven-year-old son was in the car. The convertible was decorated with a sign reading "Celebrating Family Values."

As a member of the San Francisco Board of Supervisors, Roberta took action against the Boy Scouts of America for their policy of barring homosexuals as scoutmasters. She opposed efforts by then Mayor Dianne Feinstein and city health officials to close gay bathhouses to stem the AIDS epidemic. And (we hope this wasn't a related development) she obtained city funding for a recreation and counseling center for homosexual youth. Then Roberta had the nerve to claim that Senator Jesse Helms opposed her nomination because of *anti-Semitism*. Let's run that convertible by the Wailing Wall, Bobbi, and see what kind of reaction you get.

Ira Magaziner and the Entire Task Force on Health Care

They want us all to be as healthy and long-lived as the folks in Ulan Bator and Minsk. "Managed competition" has a nice ring to it. At the horse track they call it "a boat race." You're forty-five, Ira, not getting any younger, and an intense fellow, we hear. How'd you like to have the post office perform your triple bypass?

Laura d'Andrea Tyson

The Capital Research Center has caught the chairman of Clinton's Council of Economic Advisers asserting that "there is no relationship between the taxes a nation pays and its economic performance." Hence the remarkable economic growth in the United Kingdom between the end of World War II and the election of Margaret Thatcher. Go way back and sit down, Laura.

Alice M. Rivlin

Capital Research has also tipped us to the ideology of the Office of Management and Budget's deputy director:

> Rivlin favors higher taxes, especially on energy use; a new value-added tax; and a unified state-level tax on corporations, incomes and real estate to eliminate competition for low-tax states. She argues that "claims made for the advantages of free enterprise in education have no firm basis in actual experience" and praises "centrally planned economies" because they "provide lifetime security for workers."

In the former Soviet Union they've got a word for people like Alice, and, in parts of the former Soviet bloc, Afghanistan for instance, they know what to do with them.

Michael Lerner

When it comes to cordless bungee-jumping into the abyss of bad ideas, it's hard to beat editor of *Tikkun*, Hillary guru, and general dispenser of sociopolitical meadow-dressing Lerner.

In reading Michael Kelly's enormously enjoyable Cuisinart job on the First Lady, "Saint Hillary," in the May 23, 1993, *New York Times Magazine*, we discover that Lerner pulled no punches when invited to the White House by his heavy-breathing acolyte:

> "I proposed that the Clinton Administration establish a policy where, for any proposed legislation or new program, there would have to be written first an Ethical and Community Environmental Impact Report, which would require each agency to report how the proposed legislation or new program would impact on shaping the ethics and the caring and sharing of the community covered by that agency."

Kelly lists a number of Lerner's other proposals for the Clinton administration:

These include: that the Department of Labor order "every workplace" in America "to create a mission statement explaining its function and what conception of the common good it is serving and how it is doing so"; "sponsor 'Honor Labor' campaigns designed to highlight the honor due to people for their contributions to the common good," and "train a corps of union personnel, worker representatives and psychotherapists in the relevant skills to assist developing a new spirit of cooperation, mutual caring and dedication to work."

Next stop: "Strength Through Joy."

We would kick this man but we have too much respect for our shoes. Hillary is reported to have greeted Lerner by saying, "Am I your mouthpiece or what?"

Which brings us to the Hill of Beans herself. According to syndicated columnist Don Feder, "Michael Lerner has said, 'This woman is just as smart and sensitive and morally attuned as I am.'" And we couldn't have put it better.

Yet perhaps it's time for us to reassess our opinion of *Hillary Rodham Clinton*. Of course we loathe her—who are we to disagree with her own husband? Nonetheless the First Lady has been gravely misunderstood by the right. We call her "harridan," "virago," "termagant," and "The Lady Macbeth of Little Rock." But let us examine a lickspittle piece in the May 6, 1993, Style section of the *Washington Post*. Here the slavering Martha Sherrill writes:

Way in the future, when she's old and probably legendary, Hillary Clinton wants to be able to look back and feel that she led "an integrated life," she says, sitting in her West Wing office last week. She wants to have felt unified, whole. She wants her emotional life and physical life, her spiritual life and political life all to fit together, in sync, an orchestra sitting down to play the same song.

And suddenly we realize that what we should be calling Hillary is "intellectual dust kitty." She's a bossy little rich snoot of a goody-two-shoes and not real bright who got into a fancy law school when girls were in season. Back in the sixties, the halls of academia were three deep with them.

"Hillary often quotes from an address book full of inspirational sayings and scripture," says the irony-proof Sherrill. We can hear it now: Tomorrow Is the First Day of the Rest of the Month. Michael Kelly, in his *Times Magazine* article, painted the view from Hillary's head:

The Western world, she said, needed to be made anew. America suffered from a "sleeping sickness of the soul," a "sense that somehow economic growth and prosperity, political democracy and freedom are not enough—that we lack at some core level meaning in our individual lives and meaning collectively, the sense that our lives are part of some greater effort, that we are connected to one another, that community means that we have a place where we belong no matter who we are."

She spoke of . . . a nation crippled by "alienation and despair and hopelessness," a nation that was in the throes of a "crisis of meaning."

What a chowder-skull. The idea of Hillary being the brains behind the Clinton administration is . . . very likely, come to think of it. ❖

VIII

100 Reasons Why Jimmy Carter Was a Better President Than Bill Clinton

The American Spectator, September 1993

springs

Insights compiled with the kind assistance of the patrons of the Zoo Bar on Connecticut Avenue, N.W., Washington, D.C.

1. Jimmy Carter had a nicer wife,
2. A smarter baby brother,
3. A less frightening mom,
4. And a . . . No, we can't bring ourselves to make fun of the first daughter, especially since some of us have been going through an awkward adolescent stage for nearly four decades. But we can say: "Damn it, Hillary, quit fussing with *your* hair and do something about Chelsea's."
5. And, speaking of coiffures, Jimmy Carter never in his life got a haircut that cost more than $2.50, if appearances are anything to go by.
6. Carter had governed a more important state.
7. Carter had once held a job.
8. He came from a more cosmopolitan hometown,
9. And had a more charismatic vice president.
10. It took Carter months to wreck the economy.
11. It took Carter weeks to become a national laughingstock.
12. Carter committed adultery only in his heart.
13. And, if we know anything about female tastes, Carter was telling the truth about that.
14. As for military record, Carter was, comparatively speaking, a regular Audie Murphy.
15. They were on drugs during the Carter administration—they had an excuse.
16. *We* were on drugs during the Carter administration—*we* had an excuse.
17. Carter looked—think back carefully, we promise we're telling the truth about this—less foolish in his jogging outfit.
18. Jogging actually *worked* for Carter. Say what you want against the man, he's no double-butt.
19. Carter passed out while jogging and the nation was safe for a moment.

COMPARE AND CONTRAST

Carter Administration	Clinton Administration
20. Pardoning draft dodgers	Draft dodgers
21. Women integrated into the military	Men dressed like women integrated into the military
22. Return of canal to Panama	Return of Haitians to Haiti
23. Bailout of Chrysler Corp.	Jobs in White House travel office for hick cousins from Arkansas

24. Creation of Departments of Energy and Education	Can't find enough gay disabled women of color to head the departments he's got already
25. President successfully treated for hemorrhoids	Hillary still heading health-care reform panel
26. Russians in Afghanistan	Brit Hume in White House press corps
27. Jody Powell with feet on desk	George Stephanopoulos with feet not quite touching floor
28. Kidding Mexicans about Montezuma's revenge	Kidding Mexicans about NAFTA
29. Boycott of Moscow Olympics	Not seeing much of the Bloodworth-Thomasons lately
30. Hostage rescue attempt in Iran	Trying to get Zoë Baird confirmed at Justice
31. Mount St. Helens	Air Force General Harold Campbell
32. Peace between Israel and Egypt	Peace between the FBI and IRS
33. Elvis dead	Barbra Streisand all too lively
34. SALT II	U2
35. Three Mile Island	Sam Nunn
36. Admiral Hyman Rickover	The Ty-D-Bol man
37. Wimping out in the face of the second most powerful military force in the world	Wimping out in the face of Slobodan Milošević
38. Gas shortage	Gassiest administration since who knows when
39. Mariel Boatlift	Which one is she? Does Hillary know about this one?
40. Proposition 13	(Write your own Clinton libido joke in the space provided: ____ _____)

41. Carter was a good man to have on board when your canoe was attacked by a swimming rabbit.
42. Carter hardly ever hugged or kissed anyone in public except Leonid Brezhnev.
43. The FBI didn't kill anybody at Jonestown.
44. Bert Lance could make a bigger splash doing a cannonball into the Camp David pool than Webb Hubbell.
45. Hamilton Jordan could beat Mack McLarty at arm wrestling.

46. Plus Jordan could get into Studio 54.

47. Joseph Califano was prettier than Donna Shalala.

48. And he opposed abortion (though maybe he hadn't met Donna yet).

49. Warren Christopher was young and full of pep during the Carter administration.

50. And Warren Christopher's initials look funnier on a briefcase than Cyrus Vance's did.

51. Zbigniew Brzezinski is worth more points in a Scrabble game than Anthony Lake.

52. Jimmy Carter didn't play any Fleetwood Mac songs on the campaign trail,

53. Or any Judy Collins records at home,

54. Or any saxophones anywhere.

55. **THE UNDEAD**

Carter Administration	Clinton Administration
Miss Lillian	VAT

56. No one can say a word against a Carter Supreme Court appointee.

57. Carter did not use Bloomsbury, Mayfair, Pall Mall, Hackney, Notting Hill, Shoreditch, or any other London neighborhood as the name of his child.

58. One thing about Carter-era inflation, the money may have been worthless but at least we had some.

59. **ENDANGERED SPECIES**

Carter Administration	Clinton Administration
The Snail Darter	The DLC

60. Jimmy Carter's nervous smirk was less demanding of a punch in the snoot, even if it did present a larger target.

MAJOR FOREIGN POLICY QUESTIONS

Carter Administration	Clinton Administration
61. Should Red China have a seat in the U.N.?	Is Macedonia what Macedonia is supposed to be called?
62. Does Nicaragua have strategic importance?	Is it "Ukraine" or "The Ukraine"?

63. What type of relationship with Israel best serves America's interests?	If those guys are so Jewish, how come they aren't on the staff of *Tikkun*?
64. Is it time for America to relinquish its global leadership role?	Should Chelsea go to Japan with Bill and Hillary?
65. Would economic sanctions on South Africa be effective?	How about economic sanctions on white males right here in the USA?
66. Should we sell wheat to Russia?	Let's just give them a bunch of money.
67. Is deployment of the neutron bomb immoral?	Does appointing Jean Kennedy Smith ambassador to Ireland put the Kennedys in their place or what?

68. **LANGUAGE WHICH THE PRESIDENT WOULD NOT SHUT UP IN**

Carter	*Clinton*
Spanish	English

69. Navy's football team can whip Oxford's.

WORLD VIEW
What Ideas Loomed Large Inside Their Respective Thick Skulls?

Carter	*Clinton*
70. Human rights	Partnership role for the First Lady
71. Moral equivalent of war	Partnership role for the First Lady
72. National malaise	More mayonnaise
73. Diminished expectations	David Gergen

74. Carter did not, as part of focusing his agenda, address himself as "Stupid." He let us do that for him.

75. Carter wore real blue jeans and not the Levi's 550 roomy-in-the-buns kind.

COMPARE AND CONTRAST, PART II

Carter Administration	*Clinton Administration*
76. *Mork & Mindy*	Mary Matalin and James Carville
77. *Laverne & Shirley*	Cokie Roberts and Anna Quindlen

78. *The Dukes of Hazzard* — Various half brothers
79. *Three's Company* — Gennifer Flowers
80. *Happy Days* — 1980–1992
81. *The Incredible Hulk* and *Wonder Woman* — Marriage seems stable for the moment, but super powers are fading
82. WKRP — NPR
83. *Star Wars* — Base closings
84. *Annie Hall* — Anita Hill
85. *Grease* — Mousse
86. *Saturday Night Fever* — Saturday night working late at the OEOB
87. *The Goodbye Girl* — Kimba Wood
88. *Midnight Express* — Bus trips
89. *La Cage aux Folles* — The Marines
90. *All the President's Men* — *Home Alone II*
91. Abbie Hoffman — Socks the cat

92. Carter's poll ratings were higher (in Iraq).
93. Carter walked the *whole* inaugural parade route.
94. Carter saved America from a plague of Misha the Bear Olympic mascot toys.
95. Has Bill Clinton helped the Shah of Iran get medical treatment?
96. Carter spent his time doing things like figuring out the White House tennis court playing schedule—the man *knew* his intellectual limitations.
97. Carter had enough clout to get Lani Guinier appointed to the Justice Department (and anyone who gets shot down for holding Menckenish views about the excesses of democracy has to be some kind of friend of ours even if she doesn't know it).
98. Carter let the Soviets have Angola, Ethiopia, and South Yemen. And, in retrospect, the Soviets deserved no better.
99. Carter wasn't a throwback to the Carter Era.
100. And let us not forget that Jimmy Carter gave us one thing Bill Clinton can never possibly give us—Ronald Reagan. ❖

≺ IX ≻

Why I Am
a Conservative
in the First Place

Rolling Stone, July 13–27, 1995

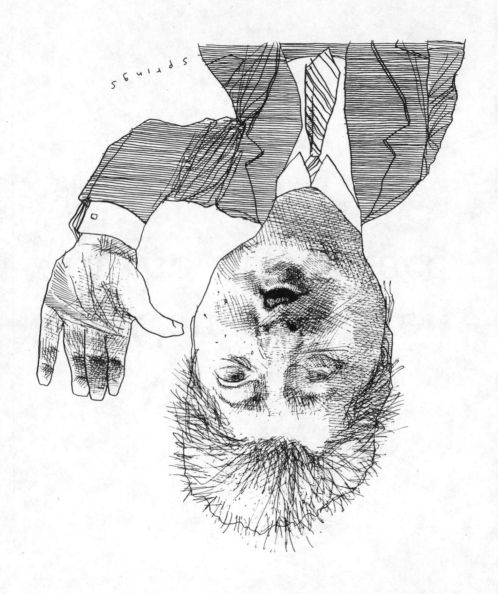

A conservative believes in the sanctity of the individual. That we are individuals—unique, disparate, and willful—is something we understand instinctively
from an early age. No child ever wrote to Santa, "Bring me, and a bunch of kids
I've never met, a pony, and we'll share." The great religions teach salvation as an
individual matter. There are no group discounts in the Ten Commandments. Christ
was not a committee. And Allah does not welcome believers into paradise saying,
"You weren't much good yourself, but you were standing near some good people."

Virtue is famously lonesome. Also vice, as anyone can testify who ever told
his mother, "All the other guys were doing it." We experience pleasure sepa-
rately. Ethan Hawke may go out on any number of wild dates, but I'm able to
sleep through them. And although we may be sorry for people who suffer, we
only "feel their pain" when we're full of baloney and running for office.

To say that we are all individuals is not a profession of selfishness any more
than it's a call to altruism. It is simply a measurement. Individuals are the units
we come in, and the individual is the wellspring of conservatism. The purpose
of conservative politics is to defend the liberty of the individual and—lest indi-
vidualism run riot—insist upon individual responsibility.

THE INDIVIDUAL AND THE STATE

The first question of political science is—or should be—What is good for
everyone? And by "everyone," we must mean "all individuals." The question
can't be, What is good for a single individual? That's megalomania—like a New
Hampshire presidential primary. And the question can't be, What is good for some
individuals? Or even, What is good for the majority of individuals? That's partisan
politics, which at best leads to Newt Gingrich or Pat Schroeder and at worst leads
to Lebanon or Rwanda. Finally, the question can't be, What is good for individuals
as a whole? There's no such thing. Individuals are only available individually.
Complete sets are not for sale.

By observing the progress (admittedly spotty and fitful) of mankind, we can
see that the things that are good for everyone are the things that have increased
the accountability of the individual, the respect for the individual, and the
power of the individual to master his own fate. Judaism gave us laws before
which all men, no matter their rank, stood as equals (though this did mean no
BLT sandwiches). Christianity taught us that each person has intrinsic worth,
Newt Gingrich and Pat Schroeder included. The rise of private enterprise and
trade provided a means of achieving wealth and autonomy other than by killing
people with broadswords. And the Industrial Revolution allowed millions of
ordinary folks an opportunity to obtain decent houses, food, and clothes (albeit

with some unfortunate side effects, such as environmental damage and Al Gore).

In order to build a political system that is good for everyone, that ensures a free society based upon the independence, prestige, and self-rule of individuals, we have to ask what all these individuals want. And be told to shut up. There's no way to know the myriad wants of diverse people. They may not know themselves. And who asked us to stick our nose in, anyway?

In a free society some people will want to make money or art or love or a mess of their lives. Some people will want to help others. Some will want others to help them. And some people will complain about how chaotic freedom is and agitate for its restriction. We can hazard certain guesses about the common desires of mankind: three squares and self-esteem. But we may find that any given example of mankind is fasting to obtain enlightenment or deeply involved in masochism.

In a free society a person can want what he likes and do what he wants to get it as long as this does not occasion real and provable harm to a fellow person (light bondage and discipline are acceptable). Thus the two fundamental rules of a political system in a free society are (1) Mind your own business; (2) Keep your hands to yourself. The political leaders of our nation would do well to reacquaint themselves with these tenets. (Hillary, mind your own business. Bill, keep your hands to yourself.)

But how do we actually go about the construction of such a political system? We don't have to. The framers of the United States Constitution have already done a fair job of it for us.

The Constitution contains a plan for representative democracy that has, over the years, been successful in luring some of our most egregious national characters out of the private sector, where they would have done no end of damage to industry and commerce, and into public office, where they can be watched.

The Constitution promulgates our system of courts and laws, the purposes of which are to keep individuals who are too smart, too big and strong, too rich, or too pretty from running the rest of us ragged. It is an imperfect system, as the O. J. Simpson trial has proved exquisitely. But it beats deciding legal cases by means of armed combat—unless you're Nicole Brown Simpson or Ron Goldman.

The Bill of Rights protects freedom of speech, freedom of religion, and freedom of assembly, of course. You could hardly call yourself free without those freedoms. But even more important, the Bill of Rights protects your money, car, house, and stereo. The Fifth Amendment says, ". . . nor shall private property be taken for public use, without just compensation." Some alleged defenders of liberty look down their noses at property rights, believing them to be the sordid, mean, and grubby side to freedom. But think how little time you spend worshiping idols your neighbors abhor or gathering in mutinous crowds. And when was the last time you said anything more controversial than "Evan Dando sucks." Now think how much time you spend using your Visa card.

In fact, most day-to-day freedoms are material freedoms. Your career, your home, your workout at the gym, shopping, traveling, entertainment, recreation, any buying and selling, any hiring and firing, the baseball team you root for, and the prerogative of its players to stay out on strike until beach volleyball becomes the national pastime are all matters of property rights. In the old Soviet Union there wasn't any private property. Everything was public—like a public restroom, which is how the old Soviet Union looked and smelled. Dead-end jobs and zoo-cage lives, shoddy goods and mucky food and constant shortages of even those, complete lack of initiative and innovation in all things—that was what made the Soviet Union so depressing, not the fact that it was illegal to stand on a street corner shouting, "Marx bites his farts!"

And one other thing the Bill of Rights does is try to protect our freedom not only from bad people and bad laws but from the vast nets and gooey webs of rules and regulations that even the best governments produce. The Constitution attempts to leave as much of life as possible to common sense or at least to local option. Says the Ninth Amendment: "The enumeration in the Constitution, of certain rights, shall not be construed to deny or disparage others retained by the people." And, continues the Tenth, "the powers not delegated to the United States by the Constitution, nor prohibited by it to the States, are reserved to the States respectively, or to the people." And it is these suit-yourself, you're-a-big-boy-now, it's-a-free-country powers that conservatism seeks to conserve.

BUT WHAT ABOUT THE OLD, THE POOR, THE DISABLED, THE DISADVANTAGED, THE HELPLESS, THE HOPELESS, THE ADDLED, AND THE DAFT?

Conservatism is sometimes confused with social Darwinism or other such me-first dogmas. Sometimes the confusion is deliberate. When those who are against conservative policies don't have sufficient opposition arguments, they call the love of freedom selfish. Of course it is—in the sense that breathing's selfish. But because you want to breathe doesn't mean that you want to suck the breath out of every person you encounter. Frankly, it's a disgusting idea and not the kind of thing the average conservative would care to be seen doing on the street.

Conservatives do not believe in the triumph of the large and powerful over the weak and useless. (Although most conservatives would make an exception to see a fistfight between Norman Schwarzkopf and George Stephanopoulos.) If all people are free, George Stephanopoulos must be allowed to run loose, too, however annoying this may be.

But some people cannot enjoy the benefits of freedom without assistance from their fellows. This may be a temporary condition, such as childhood or when I say I can drive home from a bar just fine at 3 A.M. Or, due to infirmity or affliction, the condition may be permanent. Because conservatives do not generally propose huge government programs to combat the effects of old age, illness, being a kid, or drinking ten martinis on an empty stomach, conservatives are said to be uncaring or mean-spirited. In fact, charity is an axiom of conservatism. Conservatives like and admire manners, mores, religion, family, friendship, and most fraternal and community organizations. And charity—being kind and helpful to others—is central to all these customs and institutions. Even the Crips, the Hell's Angels, and the Democratic Leadership Council claim to supply mutual aid to their members. Charity is one of the great responsibilities of freedom. But in order for us to be responsible and, hence, free, that responsibility must be personal. Of course not all needful acts of charity can be accomplished by one person. But to the extent that responsibility should be shared and merged, it should be, in a free society, shared and merged on the same basis as political power, starting with the individual. Responsibility must proceed from the bottom up, from the individual outward, never from the top down, never from the outside in, with the individual as the squeezed-cream filling of that giant Twinkie which is the state.

You have to take care of yourself to the best of your ability to do so. Your family has to take care of you. Friends have to take care of your family. Neighbors have to take care of those friends. And a community has to take care of its neighbors. Government, with its power of coercion, red tape, and inevitable unfamiliarity with the specifics of the case, is a last and a desperate resort.

There is no virtue in compulsory government charity. And no virtue in advocating it. A politician who commends himself as "caring" and "sensitive" because he wants to expand the government's charitable programs is merely saying that he's willing to try to do good with other people's money. Who isn't? A voter who takes pride in supporting such programs is telling us that he'll do good with his own money—if a gun is held to his head.

When government quits being something that we only use in an emergency and becomes the principal source of aid and assistance in our society, the size, expense, and power of that government are greatly increased. This in itself is a diminishment of the individual. And proof that we're jerks, since we've decided that politicians are wiser, kinder, and more honest than we are and that they, not we, should control the dispensation of eleemosynary goods and services.

But government charity causes other problems. If responsibility is removed from friends, family, and self, social ties are weakened. You scratch my back, and I'll get a presidential commission to investigate your claims of dorsal itch.

We don't have to look after our parents. They've got their Social Security checks and are down in Atlantic City with them right now. Our parents don't have to look after us. Head Start, a high school guidance counselor, and AmeriCorps take care of that. Our kids don't have to look after themselves. If they get addicted to drugs, there's methadone. If they get knocked up, there's welfare. And the neighbors aren't going to get involved. If they step outside, they'll be cut down by the 9mm cross fire from the drug wars between the gangs all the other neighbors belong to.

WHAT GOVERNMENT ACTUALLY CAN DO—
SUCH AS KILL PEOPLE

Making charity part of the political system confuses the mission of government. Charity is, by its own nature, approximate and imprecise. Are you guiding the old lady across the street, or are you just jerking her around? It's hard to know when to offer charity without being insulting or patronizing. It's hard to know when enough charity has been given. Parents want to help children as much as possible but don't want to wind up with helplessly dependent kids. Parents want to give children every material advantage but don't want a pack of damned spoiled brats. There are no exact rules of charity. But a government in a free society must obey exact rules, or that government's power is arbitrary, and freedom is lost.

This is why government works best when it is given limited and well-defined tasks to perform. And even the most adamantine conservative believes there are certain tasks for which government is needed. War, for instance.

Privatization of military force has been tried at various times in history. The Dark Ages in Europe are an example of the results. Law enforcement is also the proper duty of the commonwealth. As bad as our police have sometimes been, giving a Glock and a warrant to a McDonald's rent-a-cop would be worse. Certain public works and public services are best, or at least most conveniently, provided by the state. The post office, the highway system, and even schools could, perhaps, be run by corporations, but it's hard to imagine the advantage of competing networks of sewer pipes. When building a new home, you'd look up *sewers* in the Yellow Pages, call around to get the best estimate, and they'd come dig a hole to your toilet. And there are some projects that are cool—like going to the moon—but just too weird, expensive, and long-term to undertake with personal funds. Finally, there is nothing wrong with a nation acting as an ultimate insurance pool.

When catastrophes occur that individuals cannot reasonably be expected to foresee or defend themselves against, we all pitch in. It is a proper use of tax dollars to alleviate the honest distress caused by fires, floods, storms, earthquakes, riots, plagues, mudslides, and tidal waves. Although it is exasperating to the individual taxpayer when all these things happen in California every three months. I've about had it with sending Spam and tarpaulins to homeless movie producers.

There is a subtle but important difference between the government organizing mutual help in a crisis and the government providing compulsory charity—between disaster aid and a federal welfare system. Note that the end result of all the above-listed limited functions of government is simply the survival of the individual. He is protected against being attacked by Iraqis, shot by gangsters, felled by typhoid, or left to starve in his ruined Malibu, California, beach house. There is no government attempt to make his life good or fair, much less to make a good or fair person out of him.

The preamble to the Constitution says, "We, the People of the United States, in Order to form a more perfect Union, establish Justice, insure domestic Tranquility, provide for the common defense, promote the general Welfare. . . ." It doesn't say "*guarantee* the general Welfare." It certainly doesn't say "give welfare benefits to all the people in the country who aren't doing so well, even if the reason they aren't doing so well is that they're sitting on their butts in front of the TV." And here is the source of contention between conservatives and liberals. A liberal would argue that those people are watching television because they lack opportunities, they're disadvantaged, uneducated, life is unfair. And a conservative might actually agree. Conservatives do not attack liberals for saying that things are bad. Rather, the fight begins when liberals say, "Government has enormous power. Let's use that power to make things good."

It's the wrong tool for the job. The liberal is trying to fix my wristwatch with a ballpeen hammer. Government is an abstract entity. It doesn't produce anything. It isn't a business, a factory, or a farm. Government can't create wealth; only individuals can. All government is able to do is move wealth around. In the name of fairness, government can take wealth from those who produce it and give wealth to those who don't. But who's going to be the big Robin Hood? Who grabs all this stuff and hands it back out? Remember, even in a freely elected system of government, sooner or later that person is going to be someone you loathe. If you're a Republican, think about Donna Shalala. If you're a Democrat, think about Ollie North. And when government takes wealth from those who produce it, they become less inclined to produce more of it (or more inclined to hide it). And when government gives wealth to those who don't produce it, they become less productive, too, since they're already getting what they'd produce in return for not producing it.

If government is supposed to make things good, what kind of good is it supposed to make then? And how good is good enough? And who's going to decide? What person is so arrogant as to believe he knows what every other person in America deserves to get? (Well, actually, all of Washington—press and pundits included—is that arrogant. But never mind.) We don't know what people want. By the same token, we don't know what people need. The government is going to wind up giving midnight basketball to people who don't have shoes to play it in. Then there'll be a block grant to provide shoes, which people will boil because what they really lack is something to eat, and that brings us to expanding the school-lunch program. Pretty soon it's not government, it's shopping. It's not Congress and the White House, it's Mall of America. And a bunch of politicians have your charge cards.

Once the government has embarked upon a course of making all things fair, where is it to stop? Will tall people have to walk around on their knees? Will fat people be strapped to helium balloons? Will attractive people be made to wear ridiculous haircuts? (And has Tank Girl begun a one-woman campaign on this issue?)

When government quits asking, What is good for all individuals? and starts asking, What is good? individual liberty is lost. We abandon a system in which all people are considered equal and adopt a system in which all people are considered alike. Collective good replaces individual goodies. Now life will be fair at last. The whole power of government will be directed to that end. But limited government is hardly suited to a task of this magnitude. The role of government will need to be expanded enormously. Government will have to be involved in every aspect of our lives. Government will grow to a laughable size.

Or it would be laughable, except for our experience in this century. Nazi Germany, Soviet Russia, Communist China, and dozens of other places around the world did indeed create just such leviathan governmental engines of "good." And the dreadful history of the twentieth century is in large part a history of the terrible results of these collectivist endeavors. Once respect for the individual is lost, then what do a few million dead individuals matter? Especially if their deaths are for the collective good? Fifty million were killed in the war the Nazis started. Soviet purges and persecutions killed twenty million more. As many as thirty million died in Chinese famines caused by forced communization of agriculture. That's one hundred million dead from collectivism, not counting Korea, Indochina, Angola, Cuba, Nicaragua, and so on.

Of course, a liberal would say that a sharing and caring government doesn't have to turn out this way. It could be something like Sweden. And there you have it. The downside: one hundred million dead. The upside: Ace of Base, Volvos, and suicide.

WHY COLLECTIVISM DOESN'T WORK

But why can't life be more fair? Why can't Americans take better care of one another? Why can't we share the tremendous wealth of our nation? Surely if enough safeguards of liberty are written into law and we elect vigorous, committed leaders. . . . Have another hit on the bong.

Collectivism doesn't work because, first, it's based on a faulty economic premise. There is no such thing as a person's "fair share" of wealth. The gross national product is not a pizza that must be carefully divided because if I get too many slices, you have to eat the box. The economy is expandable and, in any practical sense, limitless. We have proof of this in the astonishing worldwide per-capita economic growth of the past two hundred years. Certain resources may be finite—petroleum and ocean-front property. But human resourcefulness is not. Thus we get wind power, solar power, atomic energy, gasohol, and vacations in Kansas instead of at the beach. The lesson of economic development is that what happens when we run out of a resource is what happened when we ran out of whale oil—nothing.

We're not about to run out of pizza ingredients, and if we want our fellow citizens happily shouting, "Hold the anchovies," we've got to bake more pizza. In order to do this we need economic liberty. People are much more likely to invest in expensive ovens and learn how to toss gobs of dough in the air if they stand to profit from doing so. It is for this reason that conservatives so strongly support free enterprise and capitalism, not because conservatives are greedy (although if you have any inside stock tips on companies that have invented an edible Domino's carton, this conservative would like to know).

Collectivist economic policy has been a failure the world over, but that's nothing compared with the failure of collectivist political policy. Moscovitch automobiles are bad, but even a Moscovitch doesn't collapse as spectacularly as the Berlin Wall. Collectivist political policy has failed for a very simple reason: It makes *everything* political.

Under collectivism, powers of determination rest with the entire citizenry instead of with the specific citizens. Individual decision making is replaced by the political process. Suddenly the system that elected the prom queen at your high school is in charge of your whole life.

Individuals are smarter than groups, as anybody who is a member of a committee or of a large Irish family after six in the evening can tell you. The difference between individual intelligence and group intelligence is the difference between Harvard University and the Harvard University football team.

Think of all the considerations that go into each decision you make. Is it ethical? Is it good in the long run? Who benefits? Who is harmed? What will it cost? Does it go with the couch? Now imagine a large group trying to agree on all these things—imagine a very large group, say 260 million people—and imagine that group trying to agree on every decision made by every person in the country. The result would be stupid, silly, and hugely wasteful. In short, the result would be government.

Individuals are not only smarter than groups, individuals are—and this is one of the best things about them—weaker than groups. To return to Harvard for a moment, it's the difference between picking a fight with the football team and picking a fight with Michael Kinsley.

Collectivism makes for a large and hence very powerful group. This power is centralized in the government. Any power is open to abuse. Government power is not necessarily abused more often than personal power. But when the abuse comes, it's a lulu. At work, power over the whole supply cabinet is concentrated in the person of the office manager. In government, power over the entire military is concentrated in the person of the commander in chief. You steal felt-tip pens. Nixon bombs Cambodia.

But government abuse of power does not have to be illegal, clandestine, or even abusive. Sometimes it's just a matter of the aforementioned confusion of mission. There are so many worthy national goals. And government is charged with achieving all of them. The government is supposed to strengthen the dollar but also increase export trade. The government is supposed to foster full employment but also keep inflation in check. These goals may be contradictory. There is fierce competition among their respective advocates. How can a collectivist government mediate? When the referees field a team, who calls the fouls?

Most government abuse of power is practiced openly, and much of it is heartily approved by the *Washington Post* editorial board and other such proponents of the good and the fair. But any time the government treats one person differently from another person because of the group to which that person belongs—whether it's a group of rich special-interest tax dodgers or a group of impoverished minority job seekers—individual equality is lessened, and freedom is diminished. Any time the government gives away goods and services—even if it gives them away to all people equally—individual dependence is increased, and freedom is diminished. And any time the government makes rules about people's behavior when that behavior does not occasion real and provable harm to others—telling you to buckle your seat belt or forbidding you to say *fuck* on the Internet—respect for the individual is reduced, and freedom is diminished. An individual could undertake all these things and cause no harm whatsoever and, indeed, might do some good. But the size, puissance, and ubiquitousness of government make such actions dangerous. It's one thing if I swat the dog, something else if 260 million people do.

THE WORST THING ABOUT GOVERNMENT

There is one last thing about a powerful collectivist government that is worse than everything else, and that's the person who runs it. And it doesn't matter how carefully we select our president or how carefully we select the senators and representatives who are supposed to keep that president from doing what he swore he wouldn't do. Every one of them is going to be a wrong choice. Conservatives believe in individuals. But they don't believe that individuals are good—just human. And we all know what that means. And even the best human in the world is not fit to wield the enormous power available to the modern collectivist state. To be a liberal is, ultimately, to believe otherwise. If you are a liberal and you think that there *are* people good enough to be entrusted with such awesome dominion over their fellows, I beg to remind you that Mother Teresa would be right in there with Pat Buchanan on the abortion, school-prayer, and funding-for-NEA issues.

But it's a moot point. She's not running. And neither is anybody else who's much good. The best do not rise in politics, and there are good reasons for this. The best people have jobs or, anyway, family and friends. They're too busy to spend the day going to National Church Bingo Association Play-or-Pray breakfasts, shaking hands with all the contestants in *Square-Off—The U.S. High School Geometry Olympics*. Also, all political discourse is conducted via the lowest common denominator. Notice how the extremely complex NAFTA debate quickly degenerated into "Tacos will be cheaper" versus "Mexicans carry knives." And, finally, running for office is fundamentally a matter of telling untruths. In order to get elected, a politician has to claim that the government can make you richer, smarter, taller, better looking and take six strokes off your golf game. And he has to claim that government can do all these things for free or, at least, very cheaply. As a result of these various factors, politicians are—and I'd like to put this as kindly as possible—lying, ignorant bums.

You may have what you think are excellent reasons for advocating the expansion of the powers of the state. You may have the best of intentions in desiring to limit the often reprehensible behavior of individuals. But before you declare yourself an opponent to conservatism, I ask you to think about our nation's political leaders. Would you hire any of them to cut your lawn? Dole does a tidy job, but he never gets far. He keeps wandering away to talk to the neighbors about cutting *their* lawn. Gore hasn't gotten started yet. He's talking to the cat about dandelions being an endangered species. Gingrich is using the Toro to carve out NEWT in big letters in the grass. And Clinton couldn't make up his mind whether to do the front first or the back. Should he use a push mower or the power kind? Rotary or reel? Trim, then rake? Or the other way around? Maybe fertilize and reseed instead of mowing? So he gave up, and he's inside raiding the refrigerator and flirting with your baby-sitter.

A conservative could have told you: If you want something done right, do it yourself. ❖